Instant MongoDB

Get up to speed with one of the world's most popular
NoSQL database

Amol Nayak

BIRMINGHAM - MUMBAI

Instant MongoDB

First published: July 2013

Production Reference: 1220713

Published by Packt Publishing Ltd.
Livery Place
35 Livery Street
Birmingham B3 2PB, UK.

ISBN 978-1-78216-970-3

www.packtpub.com

Credits

Author

Amol Nayak

Reviewer

Varad Meru

Acquisition Editor

Joanna Fitzpatrick

Commissioning Editor

Sruthi Kutty

Technical Editors

Dylan Fernandes

Pragati Singh

Project Coordinator

Suraj Bist

Proofreader

Aaron Nash

Graphics

Abhinash Sahu

Production Coordinator

Prachali Bhiwandkar

Cover Work

Prachali Bhiwandkar

Cover Image

Nitesh Thakur

About the Author

Amol Nayak has been working in the Java/JEE space for the past seven years and is currently employed at a leading investment bank where he is working on cutting edge technologies, predominantly open source. He is playing around with MongoDB by developing prototypes for various use cases at his workplace. He is an open source enthusiast and supports it by contributing to the open source frameworks and promoting them. He has significant ongoing contribution to the Spring Integration project, where he has worked on various adapters for JPA, XQuery, MongoDB, push notification to mobile devices, and Amazon Web Services (AWS). He has also made contributions to the Spring Data Mongo project.

I would like to thank everyone at Packt who has been involved with this book. It all started when Ashish from Packt approached me to author a starter book in Mongo. I would like to thank him for giving me this opportunity. It has an excellent experience full of learning along the way. Being my first title, I struggled initially with the process of writing and submitting the content. If it hadn't been for Suraj, Sruthi, and Yogesh from Packt, I wouldn't have been able to deliver the content on time. Suraj and Sruthi showed great patience and helped me a great deal in formatting and organizing the content that I submitted.

A special thanks to Varad Meru, the technical reviewer of the book who agreed to review the contents at very short notice. If it hadn't been for him, who reviewed the content till late at night, we wouldn't have been in a position to go ahead with the publishing of the title on time. I would like to thank the technical editor, Pragati for her exceptionally quick turnaround time which helped get the book ahead into production in no time.

Finally I would like to thank the other staff from Packt who were involved in the book's publishing process but haven't interacted with me, my office colleagues who supported me a great deal, friends, and my mom, who I wasn't able to devote much time to owing to the schedules for the delivery of the content of the book.

About the Reviewer

Varad Meru has experience in the fields of machine learning, information retrieval systems, and search engines and has worked on various projects/products ranging from core machine learning projects such as e-commerce recommender systems, e-mail analytics, and data science platforms to Cloud Infrastructure Products. He is interested in building Intelligent Systems using machine learning, data mining, data visualization, and distributed and parallel Algorithms.

He is currently working as a Software Development Engineer at *Orzota, Inc*. Previously he worked at *Persistent Systems Ltd.*, Pune as a part of the Big Data team there. He graduated from Shivaji University in 2011.

www.packtpub.com

Support files, eBooks, discount offers and more

You might want to visit www.packtpub.com for support files and downloads related to your book.

Did you know that Packt offers eBook versions of every book published, with PDF and ePub files available? You can upgrade to the eBook version at www.packtpub.com and as a print book customer, you are entitled to a discount on the eBook copy. Get in touch with us at service@packtpub.com for more details.

At www.packtpub.com, you can also read a collection of free technical articles, sign up for a range of free newsletters and receive exclusive discounts and offers on Packt books and eBooks.

packtlib.packtpub.com

Do you need instant solutions to your IT questions? PacktLib is Packt's online digital book library. Here, you can access, read and search across Packt's entire library of books.

Why Subscribe?

- ✦ Fully searchable across every book published by Packt
- ✦ Copy and paste, print and bookmark content
- ✦ On demand and accessible via web browser

Free Access for Packt account holders

If you have an account with Packt at www.packtpub.com, you can use this to access PacktLib today and view nine entirely free books. Simply use your login credentials for immediate access.

Table of Contents

Instant MongoDB

Welcome to *Instant MongoDB*. This book has been developed to provide you with all the information that you need to get started with MongoDB. You will learn the basics of MongoDB, get started by installing it, and then perform various operations on it such as inserting, updating, and querying data and discover some tips and tricks for using MongoDB.

This document contains the following sections:

So what is MongoDB? explains what MongoDB actually is, what you can do with it, and why it's so great.

Installation shows you how to download and install MongoDB with minimum effort, introducing the important configuration parameters and then how to set it up so that you can use it as soon as possible.

Quick start – setting up database and querying starts off by giving a brief comparison of terminologies from the Mongo world and their equivalent in the relational world. We then import some data in the database; this is the data we would be playing around with for most of the book. We conclude this section by connecting to the MongoDB from the Mongo shell and executing some queries to get a feel of how the queries and the data look. We basically would only be scratching the surface of this technology in this section.

Top 4 features you need to know about helps us learn how to perform various operations on MongoDB from the Mongo shell. By the end of this section you will be able to connect to a database from the shell, perform insert, update, and upsert (update + insert) operations, execute advanced queries, schema design concepts, and creating indexes for performance. Also, you will finally learn about the new aggregation framework and Map reduce operations.

People and places you should get to know lists many useful links to the project page and forums. Also, since every Open Source project is centered on a community, it provides a number of helpful articles, tutorials, and blogs which will enrich your learning process.

So, what is MongoDB?

Put simply, MongoDB is a **Documented Oriented Database**.

What is a document?

While it may vary for various implementations of different Document Oriented Databases available, as far as MongoDB is concerned it is a **BSON** document, which stands for **Binary JSON**. **JSON (JavaScript Object Notation)** is an open standard developed for human readable data exchange. Though a thorough knowledge of JSON is not really important to understand MongoDB, for keen readers the URL to its RFC is `http://tools.ietf.org/html/rfc4627`. Also, the BSON specification can be found at `http://bsonspec.org/`. Since MongoDB stores the data as BSON documents, it is a Document Oriented Database.

What does a document look like?

Consider the following example where we represent a person using JSON:

```
{
    "firstName":"Jack",
    "secondName":"Jones",
    "age":30,
    "phoneNumbers":[
       {fixedLine:"1234"},
       {mobile:"5678"}
    ],
    "residentialAddress":{
lineOne:"...",
lineTwo:"...",
city:"...",
state:"...",
zip:"...",
country:"..."
    }
}
```

As we can see, a JSON document always starts and ends with curly braces and has all the content within these braces. Multiple fields and values are separated by commas, with a field name always being a string value and the value being of any type ranging from string, numbers, date, array, another JSON document, and so on. For example in `"firstName":"Jack"`, the `firstName` is the name of the field whereas `Jack` is the value of the field.

Need for MongoDB

Many of you would probably be wondering why we need another database when we already have good old relational databases. We will try to see a few drivers from its introduction back in 2009.

Relational databases are extremely rich in features. But these features don't come for free; there is a price to pay and it is done by compromising on the scalability and flexibility. Let us see these one by one.

Scalability

It is a factor used to measure the ease with which a system can accommodate the growing amount of work or data. There are two ways in which you can scale your system: **scale up**, also known as **scale vertically** or **scale out**, also known as **scale horizontally**. Vertical scalability can simply be put up as an approach where we say "Need more processing capabilities? Upgrade to a bigger machine with more cores and memory". Unfortunately, with this approach we hit a wall as it is expensive and technically we cannot upgrade the hardware beyond a certain level. You are then left with an option to optimize your application, which might not be a very feasible approach for some systems which are running in production for years.

On the other hand, Horizontal scalability can be described as an approach where we say "Need more processing capabilities? Simple, just add more servers and multiply the processing capabilities". Theoretically this approach gives us unlimited processing power but we have more challenges in practice. For many machines to work together, there would be a communication overhead between them and the probability of any one of these machines being down at a given point of time is much higher.

MongoDB enables us to scale horizontally easily, and at the same time addresses the problems related to scaling horizontally to a great extent. The end result is that it is very easy to scale MongoDB with increasing data as compared to relational databases.

Ease of development

MongoDB doesn't have the concept of creation of schema as we have in relational databases. The document that we just saw can have an arbitrary structure when we store them in the database. This feature makes it very easy for us to model and store relatively unstructured/ complex data, which becomes difficult to model in a relational database. For example, **product catalogues** of an e-commerce application containing various items and each having different attributes. Also, it is more natural to use JSON in application development than tables from relational world.

Ok, it looks good, but what is the catch? Where not to use MongoDB?

To achieve the goal of letting MongoDB scale out easily, it had to do away with features like joins and multi document/distributed transactions. Now, you must be wondering it is pretty useless as we have taken away two of the most important features of the relational database. However, to mitigate the problems of joins is one of the reasons why MongoDB is document oriented. If you look at the preceding JSON document for the person, we have the address and the phone number as a part of the document. In relational database, these would have been in separate tables and retrieved by joining these tables together.

Distributed/Multi document transactions inhibit MongoDB to scale out and hence are not supported and nor there is a way to mitigate it. MongoDB still is atomic but the atomicity for inserts and updates is guaranteed at document level and not across multiple documents. Hence, MongoDB is not a good fit for scenarios where complex transactions are needed, such as in an OLTP banking applications. This is an area where good old relational database still rules.

To conclude, let us take a look at the following image. This graph is pretty interesting and was presented by Dwight Merriman, Founder and CEO of 10gen, the MongoDB company in one of his online courses.

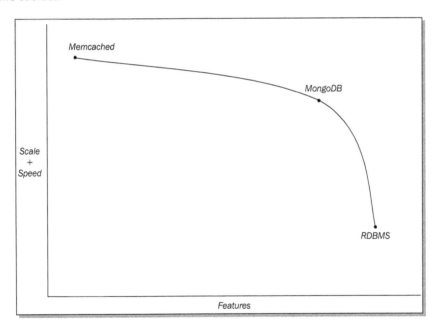

As we can see, we have on one side some products like **Memcached** which is very low on functionality but high on scalability and performance. On the other end we have **RDBMS** (**Relational Database Management System**) which is very rich in features but not that scalable. According to the research done while developing MongoDB, this graph is not linear and there is a point in it after which the scalability and performance fall steeply on adding more features to the product. MongoDB sits on this point where it gives maximum possible features without compromising too much on the scalability and performance.

Installation

In this section we will take a look at installing the MongoDB server and starting it up.

Step 1 – basic requirements

Following are the three steps you need to know or check before you start the MongoDB installation:

1. MongoDB is built to run on commodity hardware and can run on any x86 /x86_64 processor family.

2. The archive downloaded for MongoDB (2.4.3 at the time of writing this book) is about 90MB and needs around 300MB after extracting. That is the minimum you will need just to extract the archive.

3. The database files take up additional space and are pre allocated as soon as one is created. The files follow the convention <name of the database>.<running number starting from 0>. The first file allocated is of 64MB and the subsequently created files when the current data file gets full are doubled in size than the previous one but up to a maximum of 2GB, after which all files will be of size 2GB. The pre allocation of files is done in order to prevent disk fragmentation. It just fills up the file with 0 (zeros) and occupies disk space which later is used by the data that goes in the file.

 MongoDB 2.2 and above no longer supports Windows XP. You need to use newer version of Windows or use MongoDB 2.0 if you plan to continue using Windows XP. In the latter case, you will not be able to use the new features from version 2.2 onwards.

Step 2 – installing MongoDB

The installation of MongoDB is very simple. Once the binaries are downloaded, the server can be up and running in a matter of seconds.

The first step is to visit the site `http://www.mongodb.org/downloads` to download MongoDB. Always prefer the latest stable build, download the right set of binaries based on your platform. 32 bit version should only be used for development purpose only use 64 bit for production deployments. Since MongoDB uses memory mapped files for data files, the database size is restricted to a total of 2 gigabytes on 32 bit machines. The steps and screenshots I will be giving are for 32 bit Windows platform. For other platforms the steps for installation will remain same.

On Windows you can get the architecture of your platform by typing in the following command into the command prompt:

```
wmic os get osarchitecture.
```

Once the binary archive is downloaded and saved to your local disk, we need to extract it. On Windows use any file for archiving. On extracting the archive, go into the bin folder. You should see the content as shown in the following screenshot on a Windows platform. The names of the executables would be same on other platforms. mongo and mongod are the only executables we are interested in for now.

Name	Size	Date modified
bsondump.exe	10,947 KB	4/22/2013 4:02 PM
mongo.exe	6,162 KB	4/22/2013 1:43 PM
mongod.exe	10,998 KB	4/22/2013 1:55 PM
mongod.pdb	89,475 KB	4/22/2013 1:55 PM
mongodump.exe	10,980 KB	4/22/2013 2:17 PM
mongoexport.exe	10,949 KB	4/22/2013 2:43 PM
mongofiles.exe	10,962 KB	4/22/2013 3:49 PM
mongoimport.exe	10,967 KB	4/22/2013 2:57 PM
mongooplog.exe	10,946 KB	4/22/2013 3:36 PM
mongoperf.exe	10,957 KB	4/22/2013 4:16 PM
mongorestore.exe	10,972 KB	4/22/2013 2:30 PM
mongos.exe	8,588 KB	4/22/2013 2:04 PM
mongos.pdb	69,099 KB	4/22/2013 2:04 PM
mongostat.exe	10,977 KB	4/22/2013 3:10 PM
mongotop.exe	10,949 KB	4/22/2013 3:23 PM

Next, we need to start the MongoDB server by executing the mongod executable from the shell. You may add the bin folder of the extracted folder in your operating system's path variable. Let's us start by typing in the following command:

```
> mongod
```

```
C:\>mongod
mongod --help for help and startup options
Sun May 26 23:24:08.779
Sun May 26 23:24:08.780 warning: 32-bit servers don't have journaling enabled by default. Please use --journal if you w
nt durability.
Sun May 26 23:24:08.780
Sun May 26 23:24:08.794 [initandlisten] MongoDB starting : pid=7420 port=27017 dbpath=\data\db\ 32-bit host=Amol-PC
Sun May 26 23:24:08.795 [initandlisten]
Sun May 26 23:24:08.795 [initandlisten] ** NOTE: This is a 32 bit MongoDB binary.
Sun May 26 23:24:08.795 [initandlisten] **       32 bit builds are limited to less than 2GB of data (or less with --jou
nal).
Sun May 26 23:24:08.795 [initandlisten] **       Note that journaling defaults to off for 32 bit and is currently off.
Sun May 26 23:24:08.795 [initandlisten] **       See http://dochub.mongodb.org/core/32bit
Sun May 26 23:24:08.795 [initandlisten]
Sun May 26 23:24:08.795 [initandlisten] db version v2.4.3
Sun May 26 23:24:08.795 [initandlisten] git version: fe1743177a5ea03e91e0052fb5e2cb2945f6d95f
Sun May 26 23:24:08.795 [initandlisten] build info: windows sys.getwindowsversion(major=6, minor=0, build=6002, platform
2, service_pack='Service Pack 2') BOOST_LIB_VERSION=1_49
Sun May 26 23:24:08.795 [initandlisten] allocator: system
Sun May 26 23:24:08.795 [initandlisten] options: {}
Sun May 26 23:24:08.796 [initandlisten] exception in initAndListen: 10296
*************************************************************
ERROR: dbpath (\data\db\) does not exist.
Create this directory or give existing directory in --dbpath.
See http://dochub.mongodb.org/core/startingandstoppingmongo
*************************************************************
  terminating
Sun May 26 23:24:08.796 dbexit:
Sun May 26 23:24:08.796 [initandlisten] shutdown: going to close listening sockets...
Sun May 26 23:24:08.796 [initandlisten] shutdown: going to flush diaglog...
Sun May 26 23:24:08.796 [initandlisten] shutdown: going to close sockets...
Sun May 26 23:24:08.796 [initandlisten] shutdown: waiting for fs preallocator...
Sun May 26 23:24:08.796 [initandlisten] shutdown: closing all files...
Sun May 26 23:24:08.796 [initandlisten] closeAllFiles() finished
Sun May 26 23:24:08.796 dbexit: really exiting now
```

Step 3 – server fails to start

The server didn't start as we didn't provide the path for the database files on startup. By default the path used is /data/db and we don't have that folder on our file system. We can either create this directory or provide a custom location for the database.

Let's provide a custom path. Say we use c:\Mongo\Database as our database and try to start the MongoDB server once again. This time around we however provide the --dbpath parameter. So type in the following command (in your case provide the appropriate path you have chosen for the database) to start the MongoDB server:

```
> mongod --dbpath C:\Mongo\Database
```

If all goes well, the server now must have started and should be listening for connections on port **27017**. This is the default port on which the mongod process listens for new connections.

And that's it

To stop the server you can press *Ctrl + C*. This will stop the server in a clean manner.

We should not be too worried about the warning related to journaling. Since we have started the server for development purposes, we do not need journaling. Journaling is a means to ensure that the data files of the database don't go in an inconsistent state even if there is an improper shutdown of the server such as in cases of power failures. In the absence of journaling and unclean shutdown, there are bright chances that your data files will be inconsistent on restart. To know more about journaling, refer to the link http://docs.mongodb.org/manual/administration/journaling/, but don't worry if some of those things don't make much sense for now.

To know all the possible options you can provide while starting the Mongo server, use the --help option as follows:

```
> mongod --help
```

Quick start – setting up database and querying

Now let us get going with the real stuff. You must be pretty excited to have installed and started your MongoDB server quickly, right? So what is next? We will first do a quick comparison with the relational database then import data in it and execute some basic queries. Ok, so let us get started.

Step 1 – executing your first query on MongoDB

Assuming that most of us have some familiarity with the relational databases, a quick comparison of various terminologies of these two should help. Following is a table of various terms used in Relational world and Mongo world. The terms Mongo and MongoDB will be used interchangeably (I personally prefer saying Mongo over MongoDB and save the effort of typing two extra characters).

Relational world	Mongo world
Database	Database
Table	Collection
Record	Document
Column	Field
Primary Key	Primary Key
Index	Index

As we can see, except for Table, Record, and Column in relational databases, everything else means the same in Mongo.

Another big difference in relational model and Mongo is, unlike the create table for tables in relational databases, Mongo doesn't need the user to create the collections explicitly. A collection will automatically be created when the first document is inserted in it. Collections in Mongo are **schema less**. They can contain documents with disparate fields (so there is nothing stopping you from putting a document of a bicycle and a book in the same collection, one might actually do it for maintaining a product catalogue of an online store and that's the beauty of Mongo). The only field mandatory for all documents is the _id, which if not provided in the document inserted, will be automatically generated by the Mongo Server. So unlike relational databases, we simply insert documents in the collections without creating it. Inserting documents in a collection implicitly creates one. Ironically, even though Mongo is schemaless, schema designing is a crucial aspect. We will see in a later section what thought needs to be put into schema design.

Now having laid a foundation for our work and compared the relational model and Mongo, let us import some sample data into our database. This is the test data on which we would be performing various query operations. You need to download the files `IndiaCitiesPopulation.csv` and `IndiaStates.json` from `http://www.packtpub.com/support/13523`. These files contain all the cities in India whose population is above 100,000 as per 2011 census and states of India with various cities in each state respectively. There are 495 records in the CSV and 29 documents in the JSON file, not a lot of data but good enough for us to practice. You may open the files in your favorite editor and take a look at its content; the CSV file has a header and each of these headers (which are comma separated) will be used as the name of the field for each document (we have already seen in the first section how a document looks like). When we import the file, each line in the file excluding the header line, will be one document and hence we shall have 495 documents inserted in the collection. The JSON file will be imported as is with each line in the file as a separate document in the collection. You'll have to open a new terminal to execute these imports.

We shall call our database census and the collections in which the data will be imported as cities and states. Use the following command to import the data in the cities collection:

```
> mongoimport -d census -c cities --file IndiaCitiesPopulation.csv
--type csv --headerline
```

```
C:\>mongoimport -d census -c cities --file IndiaCitiesPopulation.csv --type csv --headerline
connected to: 127.0.0.1
Mon May 27 00:21:27.552 check 9 496
Mon May 27 00:21:27.554 imported 495 objects
```

The command was executed with the `.csv` file to be imported in the current directory. You can provide the absolute path of the file name too. On executing the import command the data gets imported within no time and you see the output as shown in the preceding screenshot.

Let us first see what those various command line arguments are to the `mongoimport` utility:

- ✦ `-d`: The database to which the data will be imported to. Note that we have not created a database census explicitly before importing. Similar to the collection that gets created implicitly, the database too gets created.

- ✦ `-c`: This will be the collection in the database, into which the documents will be imported. The name is arbitrary and is chosen by us; the collection gets created when we import the documents in it.

- ✦ `--file`: The file from which the documents will be imported to the collection. Only three formats JSON, CSV, and TSV are supported. In this case we are importing from a `.csv` file.

- ✦ `--type`: The default type of the input file is JSON and we need to explicitly mention the type if CSV or TSV is used. In above case we did, as the file is a `.csv` file.

- ✦ `--headerline`: Indicates that the first line in the file is the header, applicable to `.csv` and `.tsv` files only.

Now that we know what those command line arguments mean, we will try to import documents in the states collection. This is a `.json` file and the command is slightly different.

```
> mongoimport -d census -c states --file IndiaStates.json
```

This time we skip the `--type` argument as the default is JSON (so is our file) and the `--headerline` which is irrelevant for JSON files. After the import, you should have 29 objects in the `states` collection.

For our import to work, we need to have the Mongo server we started after the installation up and running. Let us connect to the database from the shell. The shell is a client application that ships with Mongo installation and will let you connect to the database and perform various operations, such as execute queries, update or insert documents, perform database administration operations, and so on. You need to execute `mongo` executable to start the shell. This executable is present in the `bin` directory of our Mongo installation. On executing Mongo, it would by default connect to the Mongo server running on localhost and would connect to the port 27017, which is the default port on which Mongo listens for new connections. On executing the command you should see a prompt which will be a `>`.

Type in `db` and hit *Enter*, we shall see the name of the database to which it is connected. The shell has a JavaScript engine and you can execute any valid JavaScript in Mongo shell. The shell has an implicit variable `db` that references the current database, `test` by default. We have our data in the `census` database. We will switch to that database by typing in the following command:

```
> use census
```

This will change the current active database to census. This means that any queries now executed from the shell will be executed on the database `census`. Typing in `db` and hitting *Enter* will confirm that the current database in use is indeed census. Next we will see what all collections are present in the current database (census that is). The command to do that is `show collections` (similarly to show all the databases you can use the `show dbs` command).

```
C:\>mongo
MongoDB shell version: 2.2.3
connecting to: test
> db
test
> use census
switched to db census
> db
census
> show collections
cities
states
system.indexes
>
```

As we see from the preceding screenshot, there are three collections in the database. The two collections `cities` and `states`, which we have created by importing the documents and a third is the `system.indexes`, which is a system generated collection used to store information about all the indexes on various collections in the database. The first operation will find the number of documents in the cities collection; we know it should be 495, let us check by executing the code.

```
> db.cities.count()
```

We should see 495 as the count which we expected. This is similar to the `select count(*)` query in a relational database. Remember, all the queries we will be executing will begin with `db.<name of the collection>` and then the function we would like to perform such as count, find, update, insert, remove, and so on. Easy, isn't it? The shell does offer us a good help. To see what possible operations we can execute on a collection, Execute the following command on the Mongo shell:

```
> db.cities.help()
```

Let us take a look at all the documents in the `cities` collection. As you must have guessed (and must be waiting to execute this), it is synonymous to executing a `select *` on a relational table without a where condition.

```
> db.cities.find()
```

Following is the result on executing the find:

```
> db.cities.find()
{ "_id" : 1, "state" : "ANDAMAN & NICOBAR ISLANDS", "city" : "Port Blair", "popu
lation" : 100608, "literates" : 81908, "sexRatio" : 889 }
{ "_id" : 2, "state" : "ANDHRA PRADESH", "city" : "Adilabad", "population" : 117
388, "literates" : 83955, "sexRatio" : 982 }
{ "_id" : 3, "state" : "ANDHRA PRADESH", "city" : "Nizamabad", "population" : 31
0467, "literates" : 221829, "sexRatio" : 1001, "isMetro" : "false" }
{ "_id" : 4, "state" : "ANDHRA PRADESH", "city" : "Ramagundam", "population" : 2
29632, "literates" : 160646, "sexRatio" : 964 }
{ "_id" : 5, "state" : "ANDHRA PRADESH", "city" : "Karimnagar", "population" : 2
60899, "literates" : 204614, "sexRatio" : 980 }
{ "_id" : 6, "state" : "ANDHRA PRADESH", "city" : "Greater Hyderabad", "populati
on" : 6809970, "literates" : 5047705, "sexRatio" : 945, "isMetro" : "true" }
{ "_id" : 7, "state" : "ANDHRA PRADESH", "city" : "Secunderabad", "population" :
213698, "literates" : 170148, "sexRatio" : 914 }
{ "_id" : 8, "state" : "ANDHRA PRADESH", "city" : "Mahbubnagar", "population" :
157902, "literates" : 119626, "sexRatio" : 988 }
{ "_id" : 9, "state" : "ANDHRA PRADESH", "city" : "Suryapet", "population" : 105
250, "literates" : 81366, "sexRatio" : 1019 }
{ "_id" : 10, "state" : "ANDHRA PRADESH", "city" : "Nalgonda", "population" : 13
5163, "literates" : 105885, "sexRatio" : 995, "isMetro" : "false" }
{ "_id" : 11, "state" : "ANDHRA PRADESH", "city" : "Miryalaguda", "population" :
103855, "literates" : 76693, "sexRatio" : 995 }
{ "_id" : 12, "state" : "ANDHRA PRADESH", "city" : "Warangal", "population" : 62
0116, "literates" : 475247, "sexRatio" : 998 }
{ "_id" : 13, "state" : "ANDHRA PRADESH", "city" : "Khammam", "population" : 184
252, "literates" : 136532, "sexRatio" : 1024 }
{ "_id" : 14, "state" : "ANDHRA PRADESH", "city" : "Srikakulam", "population" :
126003, "literates" : 97904, "sexRatio" : 1013 }
{ "_id" : 15, "state" : "ANDHRA PRADESH", "city" : "Vizianagaram", "population"
: 227533, "literates" : 169461, "sexRatio" : 1039 }
{ "_id" : 16, "state" : "ANDHRA PRADESH", "city" : "GVMC", "population" : 173032
0, "literates" : 1298896, "sexRatio" : 977 }
{ "_id" : 17, "state" : "ANDHRA PRADESH", "city" : "Rajahmundry", "population" :
343903, "literates" : 264653, "sexRatio" : 1026 }
{ "_id" : 18, "state" : "ANDHRA PRADESH", "city" : "Kakinada", "population" : 31
2255, "literates" : 231559, "sexRatio" : 1046 }
{ "_id" : 19, "state" : "ANDHRA PRADESH", "city" : "Tadepalligudem", "population
" : 103577, "literates" : 78557, "sexRatio" : 1024 }
{ "_id" : 20, "state" : "ANDHRA PRADESH", "city" : "Eluru", "population" : 21441
4, "literates" : 145516, "sexRatio" : 1028 }
Type "it" for more
> _
```

It is not difficult to guess what the query structure is. The query again starts with `db.cities` which tells that the function to be executed will be on the cities collection in the current database. The `find` function here does not accept any parameter and hence selects (finds) all the documents.

A couple of things to note here:

+ Not all documents are fetched; the shell just fetches the top 20 documents. You need to iterate to get the next 20 documents or the remaining documents in the collection, whichever is less. Now type the following command and hit *Enter*. You should see the next 20 documents (records) from the result set.

  ```
  > it
  ```

  `it` stands for iterate. It is similar to the user requesting the next page of results where it fetches the next 20 documents. If there are more in the requested result set, typing `it` will keep on retrieving the next 20 documents in the result set or the remaining number of documents whichever is less.

+ The documents are not well indented and might get difficult to read. Things become worse when we have nested documents or the documents are large. To indent the JSON document you need to invoke `.pretty()` on the result of the find. Now type in the following command and hit *Enter* to see the output:

  ```
  > db.cities.find().pretty()
  ```

Step2 – summing up and moving on

What we saw in this section is some comparison between the Relational world and Mongo world. We also imported the data in our census database, started the Mongo shell, connected to the running Mongo server and queried the collection to find the data. This process of finding the data is not powerful unless we add various conditions to it to fetch the limited set of data we wish to query. In the next section we will see a variety of operators and its combination to write powerful queries to retrieve data from Mongo. We will also see how to insert, update, and delete documents from the collection. Stay tuned for more interesting things coming up.

Top 4 features you need to know about

This section has all the meat of the content. Here we will know most of the things that a Mongo developer needs to know in his day to day work. On completing this section you should be in a good position to query, insert, update, and delete documents from the database. You will know the caveats of schema design and we will conclude by looking at the aggregation framework and Map Reduce. So, let us start off by learning about querying in Mongo.

Finding documents

One of the basic features of any database is to query it. Relational databases have a rich query language, SQL. We would expect Mongo to have its own query language too, right? And yes, it does. The queries however are represented as JSON documents and provide a rich support for querying by supporting a large number of operators. These operators can be combined to write complex queries to meet most of our requirements .I am saying most because these operators cannot perform grouping operations like the group by in relational database, there are different ways to achieve it which we will see in a later section in the book. For now, to learn and implement the query operators in the best possible way we will break this section into two:

✦ Introducing the operators one by one and learning how to use them in queries

✦ Use a combination of the operators introduced to write some complex queries on our census database

Let us now look at various operators available for finding documents in MongoDB. We will have various scenarios to run the queries on states and cities collection. It is highly recommended that you execute the queries given so that you get a good understanding of them. Let us start. I am assuming that you have the shell and Mongo server up and running. You need to be connected to the census database. As you know, you need to type `use census` on the shell to connect to it.

Let's find one and all

We start with the most basic form of query that will select all the documents. This is synonymous to `select *` of the relational database. To find all the documents in the states collection we simply use the following command:

```
> db.states.find()
```

This should print out the first 20 documents on the screen and will expect you to type `it` to continue with subsequent documents. We have seen this earlier. Now the object returned by this find is a `cursor` and you can iterate through it. Try the following command to print out just the names of each of the states:

```
> var cursor = db.states.find()
> cursor.forEach(function printEach(doc) {
```

```
print(doc.state)
  }
 )
```

There is a bit of JavaScript here. What this does is, assigns the cursor returned by `find` to a variable `cursor` in the shell. We then pass a `function` (`printEach`) with one parameter as a parameter to the `forEach` function defined in the cursor's class (yes, function as a parameter to a function). This `forEach` internally iterates through all the documents and for each of them invokes the user provided function passed as the parameter. Now all of JSON documents in the states collection have a field called `state` in them of type string. We just print that out to the console by calling `print(doc.state)`. Easy, isn't it? Don't worry if you do not know much about JavaScript. You need not be an expert in it, as and when we go through the book just pick up the concepts, which shouldn't be difficult.

Now there is another version of find called `findOne`. Type the following query in the shell:

```
> db.states.findOne()
```

You shall see it just printed out one document, the first one in the collection.

One difference between the `find` and `findOne` is that `find` returns a cursor to all documents whereas `findOne` returns the first document.

Nailing down to few documents

We are rarely interested in finding all the documents in a collection. We will like to filter the documents based on some condition; **Equal** and **Not Equal** are the most common operators we use even in the relational databases. Let us see how we can find documents where the value of some field of the document is equal or not equal to a value provided.

Say we want to find a city `Pune` in MAHARASHTRA (deliberately given in upper case as that is how it is present in the database).

The query for this is as follows:

```
> db.cities.find({city:"Pune", state:"MAHARASHTRA})
```

This is similar to the following query of Relational world:

```
select * from cities where city = 'Pune' and state ='MAHARASHTRA'
```

When multiple field values are compared as in the preceding case, the default condition is to and all values. The document will be selected when all the conditions are met. We can use the `pretty` function to indent the output console. For example, type the following query to see the document for city Pune indented which is easy to read.

```
> db.cities.find({city:"Pune", state:"MAHARASHTRA"}).pretty()
```

Similarly, the not equals operation can be implemented using the Not Equals (`$ne`) operator. Let's say we want to find all the cities other than those in the state of ANDHRA PRADESH. The Mongo query for this would be:

```
> db.cities.find({state:{$ne:"ANDHRA PRADESH"}})
```

In general whenever we want to do "field != value", we do `{field:{$ne:value}}`. For those who are seeing the queries for the first time, it may look overly complex and difficult to remember as compared to SQL in relational databases, but trust me, eventually with time when you start using these, you will get used to it and will start writing more complex queries without any difficulty.

Remember, for Not Equals we have `$ne` operator but for equals there is nothing like `$eq` operator, you simply provide the JSON with the field and value pair. Now that we have seen how Equals and Not Equals work, let us try and find city Mumbai in our collection of cities. The query is pretty simple for it and I am sure you have guessed it, right?

```
> db.cities.find({city:"Mumbai"})
```

Go ahead and execute it in the shell. What do you see? No Results!!!

Hold on, this is not possible as we have all the cities with population greater than 100000 in this collection and Mumbai definitely has to be in it. I guess the people from the census department have used some other name, but what is it? Let's see what we would have done in case this was a problem we faced in the Relational world. We would have used the `like` operator and would have written a query as follows:

```
select * from cities where lower(city) like '%mumbai%'
```

Now you'll must be saying, "We have seen and we know how to do it in a relational database, but what about in Mongo?" The answer is, we use regular expressions. To find cities with the text Mumbai in it, type and execute the following query:

```
> db.cities.find({city:/Mumbai/i})
```

```
> db.cities.find({city:/Mumbai/i}).pretty()
{
        "_id" : 233,
        "state" : "MAHARASHTRA",
        "city" : "Greater Mumbai",
        "population" : NumberLong(12478447),
        "literates" : NumberLong(10237586)
        "sexRatio" : 852,
        "isMetro" : "true"
}
{
        "_id" : 236,
        "state" : "MAHARASHTRA",
        "city" : "Navi Mumbai",
        "population" : 1119477,
        "literates" : 911542,
        "sexRatio" : 831
}
{
        "_id" : 242,
        "state" : "MAHARASHTRA",
        "city" : "Navi Mumbai Panvel Raigad",
        "population" : 194999,
        "literates" : 153608,
        "sexRatio" : 809
}
```

We have quietly added `pretty` to the query to get a pretty output, but, what we were looking for is actually named `Greater Mumbai`. Now that we have got the result, let us break down the query we wrote.

`db.cities.find` still stays the same as before and the name of the field, city is also the same as what we had executed before. What the different is this, `/Mumbai/i`. The text between leading / and trailing / is the regular expression; in this case the text `Mumbai` and everything after the trailing / is a part of regular expression options, the option `i` stands for ignore case. What we are saying in this query is, "Give me all documents that contain the word Mumbai, and yes, don't worry about the case of the string, ignore it". There is another way to provide a regex using the `$regex` operator.

Refer to the `Operator` reference in Mongo docs for more information on when to use one of the preceding forms and a complete set of options available. The link to the operator reference page is given at the end of the book.

Selecting a limited set of fields

What we have done so far is selected an entire document that matches the provided query criteria; it is just like doing a `select  *` in a relational database. How can we select only a few fields of a document?

It can be done by providing another JSON document as the second parameter to the find or `findOne` after we specify the query criteria. Let's use the same query that shows all the documents that contain the word `Mumbai` in it. Additionally we are just interested in the state and the city name.

```
> db.cities.find({city:{$regex:/Mumbai/i}}, {city:1, state:1})
```

On typing the previous query, we see the following result on the console:

```
> db.cities.find({city:{$regex:/Mumbai/i}}, {city:1, state:1})
{ "_id" : 233, "state" : "MAHARASHTRA", "city" : "Greater Mumbai" }
{ "_id" : 236, "state" : "MAHARASHTRA", "city" : "Navi Mumbai" }
{ "_id" : 242, "state" : "MAHARASHTRA", "city" : "Navi Mumbai Panvel Raigad" }
>
```

Why did we get the `_id` field? We didn't even ask for it. Well, it comes for free with other fields you have selected by default, unless you explicitly ask not to output it by adding `_id:0` to the fields to be selected. Type in the following query and check the result, the `_id` field will be absent in the result.

```
> db.cities.find({city:{$regex:/Mumbai/i}}, {city:1, state:1, _id:0})
```

Paginating and sorting documents

Let us take a look at the `sort` operation first. Let's say we want to sort the names of the cities in our cities collection by descending order of the name of the city. Type the following query in our shell to achieve this:

```
> db.cities.find().sort({city:-1})
```

The `sort` function accepts a JSON document as the parameter. The document contains all the fields that we wish to sort by and the order in which they are to be sorted, `-1` for descending and `1` for ascending. In the previous case we are sorting by just one field, the city name, in descending order. We can also choose to sort by multiple fields and the order to sort them too could be different. For example, extending the above query, say we want to sort by name of the state in descending order and within each state the cities should beordered in an ascending order of their name. Type these following lines to output the result in a format showing just the names of the states and the cities:

```
> var cursor = db.cities.find().sort({state:-1, city:1})
> cursor.forEach(function f(doc) {
  print("State: " + doc.state + ", City: " + doc.city);

  }
)
```

```
State: ANDHRA PRADESH, City: Narasaraopet
State: ANDHRA PRADESH, City: Nellore
State: ANDHRA PRADESH, City: Nizamabad
State: ANDHRA PRADESH, City: Ongole
State: ANDHRA PRADESH, City: Proddatur
State: ANDHRA PRADESH, City: Rajahmundry
State: ANDHRA PRADESH, City: Ramagundam
State: ANDHRA PRADESH, City: Secunderabad
State: ANDHRA PRADESH, City: Srikakulam
State: ANDHRA PRADESH, City: Suryapet
State: ANDHRA PRADESH, City: Tadepalligudem
State: ANDHRA PRADESH, City: Tadpatri
State: ANDHRA PRADESH, City: Tenali
State: ANDHRA PRADESH, City: Tirupati
State: ANDHRA PRADESH, City: Vijayawada
State: ANDHRA PRADESH, City: Vizianagaram
State: ANDHRA PRADESH, City: Warangal
State: ANDAMAN & NICOBAR ISLANDS, City: Port Blair
>
```

The sorting looks good. We have successfully sorted the cities collection by descending order of the state's name and ascending order of the city's name within each state. It is important to note here that the order of fields provided to the `sort` function is important. The order {state:-1, city:1} is not same as {city:1, state:-1}. Try changing the order of sort keys and see the result. The first one asks to sort by descending order of the state's name and ascending order of the city's name. There is a problem with the previous result we have printed. It printed out all the 495 cities and we can't see what is at the start of the result (well, at least my console's buffer size doesn't hold all the lines printed out). Even in real world when you display the results to the users on the front end, you show them page by page and not all together.

Let us now improve the above code to print the results in pages of 20 documents each. What we need here is to specify the "from record" and the "max number of records per page" in the query. The `skip` and `limit` functions are there to do these two things respectively. Let us rewrite the preceding code to make use of the pagination. First we will define the function that prints out the values and assign it to a variable `func`; this is the same function we defined previously, inline to the `forEach` function. We write it down again.

```
> func = function f(doc) {
        print("State: " + doc.state + ", City: " + doc.city);
  }
```

Let's get a cursor of the first 20 documents and then print all of them using the function defined previously. Since we want the first 20 documents we may choose to leave out the `skip` function. By default if skip is not specified, the documents are fetched from the first one.

```
> var cursor = db.cities.find().sort({state:-1, city:1}).limit(20)
```

```
> cursor.forEach(func)
```

What's different in it than the previous queries is that there is an additional function call `limit` with the number of items to display as the parameter to it. Execution of the previous two statements will give us an output as shown in the following screenshot:

```
> var cursor = db.cities.find().sort((state:-1, city:1)).limit(20)
> cursor.forEach(func)
State: WEST BENGAL, City: Asansol
State: WEST BENGAL, City: Ashokenagar Kalyangarh
State: WEST BENGAL, City: Baharampur
State: WEST BENGAL, City: Baidyabati
State: WEST BENGAL, City: Bally
State: WEST BENGAL, City: Bally
State: WEST BENGAL, City: Balurghat
State: WEST BENGAL, City: Bankura
State: WEST BENGAL, City: Bansberia
State: WEST BENGAL, City: Baranagar
State: WEST BENGAL, City: Barasat
State: WEST BENGAL, City: Barddhaman
State: WEST BENGAL, City: Barrackpur
State: WEST BENGAL, City: Basirhat
State: WEST BENGAL, City: Bhadreswar
State: WEST BENGAL, City: Bhatpara
State: WEST BENGAL, City: Bidhan Nagar
State: WEST BENGAL, City: Bongaon
State: WEST BENGAL, City: Champdani
State: WEST BENGAL, City: Chandannagar
>
```

Looks good, this printed out first 20 documents. Now let us print the next 20. We will use `skip` method this time around as we want to skip the first 20 documents and get the next 20 from 21st document onwards. We type in the following statements to show the next 20 documents:

```
> var cursor = db.cities.find().sort({state:-1, city:1}).skip(20).
limit(20)
```

```
> cursor.forEach(func)
```

I am assuming that so far you are with me and executing things as and when we discuss. If you find something difficult, read again and try to understand the concept. Ok, getting back to the preceding executed statements. The output for it is as expected and should print documents from the 21st document onwards till document number 40.

If you carry on for more pages, you will be printing just 15 documents on the last page starting from document id 481. If you provide a value to skip that is more than the total number of documents, no exception will be thrown. Just no documents will be returned by the query.

Yet more comparison operators

Though Equals, Not Equals, and Regular expressions are sufficient for many requirements, we at times need to compare the values using the `less than, less than or equal to, greater than`, and `greater than or equal to` operators. We will now see how to use them in our Mongo query language. Let us say we want to find all the cities where the sex ratio is less than 800. The query for this in Mongo would be as follows:

```
> db.cities.find({sexRatio:{$lt:800}})
```

The operator for Less Than is `$lt` and for Less Than or Equal to is `$lte`. The query is same as the condition `sexRatio < 800` in SQL for a relational database.

In general, whenever you want to do a field less than value in Mongo, you will do as follows:

```
{field:{$lt:value}
```

It is similar for Less than or equal to as well. Greater Than and Greater Than or Equal to is not different from the above two operators and you might have guessed that they are `$gt` and `$gte` respectively. Let us use Greater Than or Equal to, to find all the cities whose population is greater than or equal to 10 million (10,000,000). The query to get these cities is as follows:

```
> db.cities.find({population:{$gte:10000000}})
```

An important thing to note is that a collection can have documents with different fields. Not all fields might be present in all documents, thanks to the schemaless nature of the collections in Mongo. What do you think will happen when we use such field with these `$lt`, `$lte`, `$gt`, or `$gte` operator? Mongo just will not return documents without the field used for comparison in the result. It will just include the documents which contain the field used in the condition and the value of that field satisfies the condition in the provided query. We won't face this problem in our cities collection as all the documents have same fields in them.

We have three more operators `$in`, `$nin`, and `$all` that should complete what we call the comparison operators. Let us start with the In operator. If we recall from the Relational world, we have an In operator which can be used to find all the rows where the value of a particular column is in a particular set of values given. The In operator of Mongo is not different from its relational counterpart; it has the same semantics. Let us write a Mongo Query that will find the cities with name Kolkata and Chennai. The query for this is as follows:

```
> db.cities.find({city:{$in:["Kolkata", "Chennai"]}})
```

That's it. You still haven't seen the coolest part. What do you think of the query below?

```
> db.cities.find({city:{$in:["Kolkata", "Chennai", /Mumbai/]}})
```

This query not only includes two cities `Kolkata` and `Chennai`, but also includes all the cities that match the given regular expression `/Mumbai/`. It's like combining In and the Like operator together which doesn't work in relational database (you need to work around using or conditions for this). Since Mongo collections are schema less and the fields can contain values which are arrays, we need to consider two more things when using the `$in` operator. If the field used in the In operator is not present in the document, the document is not selected. So only those documents containing the field and whose value is present in the set of values provided are selected. Another case is when the field is of the type `array`, in this case the document will be selected if any of the values in the array match at least one value in the set provided to the In operator.

There is no prize for guessing that the Not In operator is `$nin` and what it does. Let's quickly see one example though. Let's say we want to find a count of all cities except those in the state of MAHARASHTRA and KARNATAKA. Our query for it would be as follows:

```
> db.cities.find({state:{$nin:["MAHARASHTRA", "KARNATAKA"]}}).count()
```

If we however have a case where the field we use with the `$nin` operator is not present in all the documents, then the documents not having this field will be selected as well. This is something you need to watch out. If you do not want these documents to be returned, then you have to check for the existence of the field in the document along with the `$nin` operator. The existence of a field in the document is checked using the `$exists` operator, which we will see soon.

Finally we take a look at the All operator `$all`. The all operator can be used to check if a field in a document has all the values specified in the query. Though it is legal to use on any type of field, it really makes sense to use this operator of fields of type array, since arrays are the only types which can hold multiple values at the same time. Let's say we want to find the state which has both the cities Pune and Thane. The query for that would be as follows:

```
> db.states.find({cities:{$all:["Pune", "Thane"]}})
```

As we mentioned earlier, `$all` operator can also be used on fields which contain single value. For example the query `db.cities.find({city:{$all:["Pune"]}})` is perfectly valid and will return us one document, but using `db.cities.find({city:"Pune"})` is more intuitive and definitely a preferred option. Thus it makes sense on fields of type array only.

Simple, isn't it? We have made good progress already and if you have tried out all the queries we have seen so far, which I am sure you have, then you are in a good position to write quite a substantial number of the queries using all the possible comparison operators, which should suffice for most of the use cases.

Checking for the existence of a field

Before we move ahead, let's take a look at the `$exists` operator. The Exists operator will check for the existence or non existence of a particular field in a document. This is an interesting operator and has no operator similar to it in the Relational world. This operator exists because of the schema less nature of Mongo. Let us say that we want to find all states that do not have other information on them (the `info` field will be absent in the document). The query for that is as follows:

```
> db.states.find({info:{$exists:false}})
```

This query is self-explanatory. All it does is selects all the documents where the `info` field is not present in the documents in the collections. The `$exists` with the boolean value of true will return all the documents containing the mentioned field irrespective of its value. It will even select those documents where the value of this field is null. It is important to note that this operator is *not* meant to select/exclude documents with null values of fields.

Getting logical

We now look at a few logical operators that can be used to perform the `and`, `or`, `not`, and `nor` conditions. If you have observed carefully all our queries, then you must have seen we have never used any of the logical operators. Let us take this query which we have seen earlier, as an example:

```
> db.cities.find({city:"Pune", state:"MAHARASHTRA"})
```

What we intend to do in this query is to find a city whose name is Pune and the state is MAHARASHTRA. Did we specify the `and` condition in the above query? No, we didn't. We need not add one but it is implicit. The preceding query can also be expressed as follows:

```
> db.cities.find({$and:[{city:"Pune", state:"MAHARASHTRA"}]})
```

This is done by making use of the `$and` operator. The operator is expressed as `{$and:[expression1, expression2 … expressionN]}`, where the evaluation of the next expressions stop if any of them evaluate to false.

You may be wondering why do we need the `$and` operator? The original query without the operator looks simple. You will appreciate the existence of this operator when you see the scenario that we look at next. If you observe the `cities` collection carefully, we have a field called `isMetro` in some documents whose value is true or false. While it is absent in some documents. Let's say we execute the following query:

```
> db.cities.find({isMetro:{$ne:"true"}}).count()
```

We get 487 cities. Clearly it shows that 8 cities (we have 495 in all) are metro cities. Of the 487 cities not all have the `isMetro` field. So let us check the existence of this field and see how many cities we have which have this field present and is set to false. Basically we plan to find all the documents that have the `isMetro` field but the value is not true.

We do so by amending the above query and add an $exists operator, which we saw earlier.

```
> db.cities.find({isMetro:{$exists:true}, isMetro:{$ne:"true"}})
```

This query looks good doesn't it? We are saying the field isMetro exists and its value is not equal to true. Let's execute it. On execution, following are some of the documents in the result:

```
{ "_id" : 18, "state" : "ANDHRA PRADESH", "city" : "Kakinada", "population" : 31
2255, "literates" : 231559, "sexRatio" : 1046 }
{ "_id" : 19, "state" : "ANDHRA PRADESH", "city" : "Tadepalligudem", "population
" : 103577, "literates" : 78557, "sexRatio" : 1024 }
{ "_id" : 20, "state" : "ANDHRA PRADESH", "city" : "Eluru", "population" : 21441
4, "literates" : 145516, "sexRatio" : 1028 }
{ "_id" : 21, "state" : "ANDHRA PRADESH", "city" : "Bhimavaram", "population" :
142280, "literates" : 108535, "sexRatio" : 1031 }
Type "it" for more
```

WHOA!! Something has gone wrong; we weren't expecting documents that don't contain the isMetro field. Then how come they are present in the result? If you look at the query again, we have used the isMetro field twice in two different conditions. Once for checking its existence and another for checking if its value is not equal to true. This doesn't give you the result you expect. The query processor will only consider the last condition for a given field, in this case it is the $ne operator. It will disregard the exists operator. The $and operator comes to the rescue in this situation. You can change the previous query to the following query:

```
> db.cities.find({$and: [{isMetro:{$ne:"true"}},
{isMetro:{$exists:true}}]})
```

After execution of the preceding query the output should look good. In this case the two conditions on isMetro field are two separate expressions of the and operator and hence it works fine. This was an extremely important thing to remember when writing a query.

 Do not use the same field multiple times for multiple conditions in the same query as we did earlier. This will yield unexpected results.

There is however another way to achieve it and still not use the $and operator. In cases like the one we just saw, where you want to use the same field multiple times, the query can be written as follows:

```
> db.cities.find({isMetro:{$ne:"true", $exists:true}})
```

Ok, enough with the And operator. Let's see the Or operator now. Or is another commonly used boolean operator in queries. Not surprisingly it is $or. Its usage is also identical to the $and operator. It is also a short circuit operator like And operator where if any of the expression evaluates to true, rest of the expressions are not evaluated. Let us quickly see an example usage of it on our collection.

Let's find all the cities in ASSAM or NAGALAND. The query for that is:

```
> db.cities.find({$or: [{state:"ASSAM"}, {state:"NAGALAND"}]})
```

We will look at two more logical operators, Not and Nor operator, we will just scratch the surface for these two operators and move on. Personally I don't think these operators will be used quite often. Nevertheless, let us see an example of their usage. The not operator will select all documents where the expression specified on a particular field of the document does not match. A document will be selected even if the provided field is not present in it.

Let us find the count of cities where the population is greater than 1 million.

```
> db.cities.find({population:{$not:{$lte:1000000}}}).count()
```

Well, for this operation we really do not need the Not operator and can simply be achieved using `db.cities.find({population:{$gt:1000000}}).count()`.

There is one big difference though in both the queries. Try changing the field `population` in the query to something else that doesn't exist in the document. For example, use the following query:

```
> db.cities.find({nonExistent:{$not:{$lte:1000000}}}).count()
```

and

```
> db.cities.find({nonExistent:{$gt:1000000}}).count()
```

You should see that the query using $gt gives the count zero whereas the one using $not gives the count 495, that is selects all the documents. Why did this happen? It is simply because the Not operator will select a document if the given field is not present in the document whereas $gt operator doesn't. The choice of what operator to use is very crucial when querying using a field of the document which is not present in all the documents in a collection. We really don't need to consider this in a relational database as the column will be there for each and every row in a table. But in Mongo, remember that the collections are schema less.

The Nor operator will select a document if all the expressions given in the query do not match for the document, or the field used in the expression is not present in the document. But remember, all expressions should not match a document for it to be selected.

Let us find the count of all cities not in MAHARASHTRA and UTTAR PRADESH having population of 1 million and above (that is greater than or equal to 1 million).

```
> db.cities.find({$nor:[{population:{$lt:1000000}},{state:"MAHARASHTRA"},
{state:"UTTAR PRADESH"}]}).count()
```

This will select all the documents where all the three conditions given in the query, for the population less than 1000000, state equals MAHARASHTRA, and state equals UTTAR PRADESH will be false. The query can be also be expressed in terms of $and, $gte, and $ne operators and the result will be identical. Since now you know all the operators, go ahead and give it a shot; see if the counts of the documents you get with the preceding query and the one you write are same. The results will vary in case the documents have disparate fields, and, those are used in query expressions as we have explained in the $not operator.

Accessing the nested fields

How many of you have observed so far that all the queries we have used are using fields at the top level in a document? I am sure you have, right? Let us try and find the state whose capital is Mumbai. The query sounds simple isn't it? But there is a small challenge. If you look closely into the `states` collection, the capital is not mentioned in all the documents and wherever it is given, it is in the inner document with field name `info` and the field within the document is called `capital`. The info field's value in documents looks something as follows:

```
"info" : {
        "neighbouringStates" : [

            ...
        ],
        "area" :...
        "capital" : ...,
        "largestCity" : ...
    }
}
```

So how do we find the state with its capital's city as Mumbai? It is simple, you simply type in the following query:

```
> db.states.find({"info.capital":"Mumbai"})
```

In the preceding command we accessed the nested field using `info.capital`, which denotes that the `capital` field is nested in the top level field info's value. You may access a field to any level in such a manner.

The leftover operators

Phew, we have seen quite a lot of operators and it is getting difficult to remember these, isn't it? Don't worry though; once you start using them regularly you will get a good grip of them and they will look easy eventually. To make things slightly better we will have a section later where we will try putting most of the operators to use. But before we reach that section, let us take a look at the few remaining operators.

The `type` operator will select all the documents where the type of a field is one of the mentioned BSON fields. There is a number associated with each type and we won't be showing it here. You can take a look at the Operator Reference page of MongoDB at `http://docs.mongodb.org/manual/reference/operator/type/#_S_type` for more information on various types available. Let us put the type operator to use. We know that the info field in the state's document has a value and it is a JSON document with some information given on all the states. The `capital` field in this nested document is a string which is the capital city of the state. Let us see if there is a document present in the collection whose `capital` field has a value other than string. The query will basically check for the existence of the capital field and then if it does, will check if its value is something other than string. The number representing string type is 2.

The query to find such a state is as follows:

```
> db.states.find({"info.capital":{$exists:true, $not:{$type:2}}})
```

The query uses a combination of using nested field, `$exists` operator, `$not` operator, and the `$type` operator. In plain English, it is like saying "`info.capital` field exists and its type is not equal to string".

If you execute the previous query from the shell you will see there is a state that has a value for the `capital` field which is not a string but it is another document. I have done this for two reasons:

✦ Demonstrate the usage of the `$type` operator

✦ Convey that what we have done here is a bad practice and is highly discouraged

Though MongoDB is schema less and doesn't enforce any type to a particular field, it is a bad practice to have values of different types for a field in different documents of the same collection. All other documents having the capital field have values of type string. A better approach would be to have two separate fields, say, `summerCapital` and `winterCapital` and not have the capital field at all in the document (the inner one which is the value of the info field) or rename the field as capitals. The application reading the document from the database however has to handle this condition in either cases. We will fix this problem later when we see how to update documents.

The size operator (`$size`) is used to select the document based on the size of the array. In my opinion this isn't a very powerful operator and can only be used to check if the given array size is equal to a value or not. You will see what I mean. Let's try and find all the states that are bordering with 3 countries. To do this we simply have to check if the array in field `neighbouringCountries` of the info document has size 3 or not. The query will be as follows:

```
> db.states.find({"info.neighbouringCountries":{$size:3}})
```

Executing this should get you one state, WEST BENGAL. So far it sounds good. Now let us try to find the states that are bordering with 2 or more states. Unfortunately we cannot write this query using the `$size` operator. The recommended way is to introduce another field which will be an integer value that will hold the size of the `neighbouringCountries` field's array. This field should be updated by the application on addition or deletion of values from the array whose size it holds. If you introduce this field then you might never need to use the `$size` operator assuming this value is consistent with the actual size of the array and that is why I feel this operator might not be too widely used. What's more? The query cannot use an index for `$size` portion. We however can have an index over the number field which holds the size of the array and lets us query efficiently. Flip side is that the application is responsible for the consistency of this field with the size of the array but that's not too much of an effort.

We finish off with the slice operator (`$slice`). When we select a particular document and the document has a field of type array, it will fetch the entire array. There could be too much of data to be retrieved or we might not be interested in all of them. The slice operator lets us retrieve what we exactly want. Look at this operator as a way to paginate the inner array type fields. Let us consider the previous query again, which found the state bordering 3 countries. The query is as follows:

```
> db.states.find({"info.neighbouringCountries":{$size:3}})
```

This query also fetched a big list of cities in the `cities` array though we are not interested in the cities. Suppose we want the top 5 cities, we would do the following:

```
>db.states.find({"info.neighbouringCountries":{$size:3}},
    {"cities":{$slice:5}})
```

Take a look at: `http://docs.mongodb.org/manual/reference/projection/slice/#prj._S_slice` for more details on the slice operator. You can find ways to get the bottom *n* elements of an array or some intermediate members of the array.

Putting it all together

Now finally is the time to look at using some of these operators together. We shall look at a scenario and then write queries to retrieve data for it after doing some analysis.

Scenario

We need to print out to the console a small report containing few details. The requirement is to get the name of the city, state, population, and sex ratio of all the metros (those in our database). Additionally we have to fetch the same details for top 3 most populous non metro cities in 3 largest states in terms of area. The output is expected in this format with cities printed in descending order of their population.

```
City     State     Population     Sex ratio
-----------------------------------------------------------------
city 1   state 1   population 1   ratio 1
city 2   state 2   population 2   ratio 2
city n   state n   population n   ratio n
```

Analysis

This might be slightly complex for a newbie in JavaScript but I will try to explain each and every line of the code we will write down. Let us first analyze the above statement and see how we can extract the required details. Looking at the fields we can extract all of them from the cities collection. However to extract the three largest states we will need to query the states collection too. Also, looking at the preceding output format required it is clear that we will need a small JavaScript code along with the queries. First we try to get the counts and get an idea of the number of results we can expect. We start by looking at the number of metros in our database.

Execute the following query to find the result:

```
> db.cities.find({isMetro:"true"}).count()
```

This gives us a count of 8. Adding 9 to this which would be for 3 most populous non metro cities each from 3 largest states, we should have a total of 17 records in our report. We now write a JavaScript function that would extract the report for us in the required format.

```
function printReport() {
  //1 Top 3 states in terms of area
  var largestStates = db.states.find({}, {state:1, _id:0}).
sort({"info.area":-1}).limit(3)

  //2 Top 3 populous non metros in largest states
  var populousCities = []
  var i = 0
  while(largestStates.hasNext()) {
    var mostPopulousCities = db.cities.find(
       {state:largestStates.next().state, isMetro:{$ne:"true"}}
     )
     .sort({population:-1})
    .limit(3)

    while(mostPopulousCities.hasNext()) {
      populousCities[i++] = mostPopulousCities.next().city
    }
  }
  //3 Find the final list of cities
  var finalCities = db.cities.find({$or:[{isMetro:"true"},
{city:{$in:populousCities}}]}).sort({population:-1})

  print("City\t\t\tState\t\t\tPopulation\t\t\tSex Ratio")
  print("--------------------------------------------------------
-------------------------------------------")
  while(finalCities.hasNext()) {
    var finalCity = finalCities.next()
    print(finalCity.city + "\t\t\t" + finalCity.state + "\t\t\t" +
finalCity.population + "\t\t\t" + finalCity.sexRatio)
  }
}
```

Let us understand this piece of code. We have put in checkpoints in our code with some numbers as comments. We will be looking at the code and explaining what each of these lines do. Let's first look at the code between 1 and 2.

This query selects all states but just selects the state field, the field holding the name of the state from each document selected. Additionally, it sorts them by descending order of their area and limits the result to top 3 results. This then achieves the goal of finding the 3 largest states by area. Moving on and looking at the piece of code between 2 and 3.

This initializes an array to an empty array which will be used to hold the most populous non metro cities in the three largest states and a variable initialized to zero. The loop after initialization will iterate through the three largest states and for each of them fire one query in the cities collection where the state is same as the one in the current iteration of the loop and the city is not a metro. The cities again will be sorted by their population in descending order and limited to the top three results. This will achieve our goal of finding the top 3 populous non metro cities in the 3 largest states by area. For each query executed we iterate through all the 3 cities and add their names to the populousCities array.

The portion of the code after comment 3 simply executes another query on the cities collection where we select the city if it is a metro or if the city name is present in the populousCities array we populated earlier. The final bit just iterates through the cursor returned and prints the result out with a lot of tabs (\t) between each column. Do not bother much for the alignment of the result printed. The result printed out to the console looks like the following screenshot. The above typed code can then be directly pasted to the shell and the printReport function invoked.

```
> printReport()
City                         State                     Population              Sex Ratio
------------------------------------------------------------------------------------------
Greater Mumbai                    MAHARASHTRA               12478447                    852
DMC                          NCT OF DELHI        11007835                    875
Greater Hyderabad                 ANDHRA PRADESH              6809970                   945
Chennai                      TAMIL NADU          4681087                 986
Kolkata                      WEST BENGAL         4486679                 899
Surat                        GUJARAT       4462002                758
Pune                         MAHARASHTRA         3115431                 945
Jaipur                       RAJASTHAN           3073350                 898
Kanpur                       UTTAR PRADESH       2767031                 842
Nagpur                       MAHARASHTRA         2405421                 961
Indore                       MADHYA PRADESH      1960631                 921
Thane                        MAHARASHTRA         1818872                 882
Bhopal                       MADHYA PRADESH      1795648                 911
Pimpri-Chinchwad                  MAHARASHTRA                1729359                    828
Jabalpur                          MADHYA PRADESH             1054336                   929
Jodhpur                      RAJASTHAN           1033918                 900
Kota                         RAJASTHAN           1001365                 890
> _
```

That takes care of the report needed and we have successfully applied some of our knowledge around querying the collections to extract the data out of them.

Inserts, updates, and upserts

We have so far seen a lot on how to query data from MongoDB. We will now see how to perform inserts and update the data in Mongo. Inserts are in fact very simple and there is not much to see. Let's start by adding a state SIKKIM to the states collection. Since the maximum value of the _id in the states collection is 29, we assign the value 30 to this one. Start by creating a document for the state as follows:

```
> var state = { _id:30, state:"SIKKIM"}
```

What we have done here is create a new variable in the shell called `state` and assigned it a document for the Sikkim state. We have explicitly chosen the value 30 for `_id` field as not providing one will generate a default value on insert of the document by the Mongo server. To insert this document execute the following on the Mongo shell:

```
> db.states.insert(state)
```

And that's it, we now have the state's document created. To double check let us query the states collection for Sikkim. Executing the following query should give you one document. If it does then all is fine and we have successfully inserted the document in the collection.

```
> db.states.find({state:"SIKKIM"})
```

Now that we have a state, let us add some cities to it. We have the field called cities whose value is an array. We start by adding the capital of the state, Gangtok. Before we execute any update let us backup the state's document (you will soon see why).

```
>var sikkim = db.states.findOne({state:/sikkim/i})
```

Now let's go for the update, execute the following script to perform an update operation on the document:

```
> db.states.update({_id:30}, {cities:["Gangtok"]})
```

Now, let us query the states collection to see the result. Execute the following query:

```
> db.states.find({_id:30})
```

This is what we see

```
> db.states.update({_id:30}, {cities:["Gangtok"]})
> db.states.find({_id:30})
{ "_id" : 30, "cities" : [ "Gangtok" ] }
> _
```

Huh?? What happened? Weren't we expecting to just update the cities field of the document? Isn't this what we do in a relational database, just provide the values to update and a where condition? Let's look at the update once again:

```
> db.states.update({_id:30}, {cities:["Gangtok"]})
```

The first part of the update is straightforward and is the criteria to match the document(s). The second one is bit tricky; it is the document that will replace the entire existing document and not an incremental update as we might expect. All the fields provided here will replace the existing fields except the `_id` field, which is immutable of the existing document. That is the reason why we lost the field state. Fortunately we have a backup of the original document. Let us modify this document to add the cities array to the state with one city in it. Execute the following code to achieve this:

```
> sikkim.cities = ["Gangtok"]
```

You may see what the document looks like by typing in `sikkim` on the command prompt and hit *Enter*. Let's update it back. Execute the following update:

```
> db.states.update({_id:30}, sikkim)
```

On querying the database we see that the state's document is as we had expected it to be. But hold on; are we saying to update just one field we need to provide the entire document? Things get worse if the document is big. It just doesn't sound right. Isn't it?

Update operators to our rescue

Let us start off by the setting a field of a document. We use the same document for state Sikkim and add to it some info. We will first set the capital of the state. Execute the following update:

```
> db.states.update({state:"SIKKIM"}, {$set:{info:{capital:"Gangtok"}}})
```

This simply sets a new field called `info` in the document for state `SIKKIM` whose value is another document. Go ahead and query for the state in the states collection, you shall see the result is as expected and should now contain the newly added field `info`. Similarly the `unset` operator is used to unset a field from the document. This will take the field off from the document alogether. Let us try using it with the `info` field.

```
> db.states.update({state:"SIKKIM"}, {$unset:{info:""}})
```

If you query for the document again, you will see the info field is now gone. Do put it back again using the `$set` operator we saw earlier. As you must have observed the value of the field info in the unset operation is irrelevant we have provided an empty text and yet the field is removed. The field will be removed irrespective of the value.

Another interesting operator is the `rename` operator; it can be used to rename the value of a field atomically. Do you remember we came across a situation where the value of the capital field of the info document is not a string value but another document and we said such design is highly discouraged? Well, if you don't remember you may skim back few pages and look for the page where we introduced the `$type` operator. First execute the following query to see that state's document. Take a note of the `_id` field as we will be using it to query for this document later after executing the rename operation.

Just to recap, the following query finds the document for the state that has the field `info.capital` but not of type string.

```
> db.states.find({"info.capital":{$exists:true, $not:{$type:2}}}).pretty()
```

```
> db.states.find({"info.capital":{$exists:true, $not:{$type:2}}}).pretty()
{
        "_id" : 10,
        "state" : "JAMMU & KASHMIR",
        "cities" : [
                "Srinagar",
                "Anantnag",
                "Jammu"
        ],
        "info" : {
                "neighbouringStates" : [
                        "PUNJAB",
                        "HIMACHAL PRADESH"
                ],
                "neighbouringCountries" : [
                        "PAKISTAN",
                        "CHINA"
                ],
                "area" : 222236,
                "largestCity" : "Srinagar",
                "capital" : {
                        "summerCapital" : "Srinagar",
                        "winterCapital" : "Jammu"
                }
        }
}
>
```

We have decided that we rename the `capital` field of the document given in the `info` field to value capitals as this would mean that all the documents in the collection will then have the type of the `capital` field as a string. Let us use the rename operator to achieve this:

```
> db.states.update({"info.capital":{$exists:true, $not:{$type:2}}},
{$rename:{ "info.capital":"info.capitals"}})
```

The update statement is self-explanatory; it just renames the field `info.capital` to `info.capitals`, which matches the query provided to the update. Execute the following query and see the result:

```
> db.states.find({_id:10}).pretty()
```

The field `capital` would have been renamed to `capitals`.

We will now look at array operators and start by adding a new city to the array of cities in the Sikkim state's document. The document for the state currently looks like the following code:

```
{ "_id" : 30, "cities" : [ "Gangtok" ], "info" : { "capital" : "Gangtok"
}, "state" : "SIKKIM"}
```

Let us see the `$push` operator first, which will add another city to the cities array. The general form of the push operator is as follows:

```
db.<collection>.update(<query>,{$push:{<array field to push to>:<value to
push>}})
```

We want to add a new city, Pelling, to the cities array in the state's document and we achieve it using the following update:

```
>db.states.update({_id:30}, {$push:{cities:"Pelling"}})
```

On querying you shall see that the cities array has one more city and now has two of them in all. The $pushAll operator is similar to the $push operator but is used to push multiple elements to the array at a time. The value in this case will be an array instead of the string used in push. The following update will add two more cities, Gezing and Mangan, to the cities array:

```
> db.states.update({_id:30}, {$pushAll:{cities:["Gezing","Mangan"]}})
```

The $push and $pushAll operators are however not idempotent, meaning, on executing the update multiple times the same cities will be duplicated in the cities array. To ensure that the update is idempotent there is an operator $addToSet. The operator is same as $push except that the given value will not be added to the array if it already exists, thus making multiple updates using $addToSet idempotent. We are not showing its usage here but you may give a try to add a new city using $addToSet and execute the update multiple times. Try doing the same with the push operator.

To remove values from an array, we have the $pop, $pull, and $pullAll operators. The $pop operator can be used to remove elements from the head or tail of an array. Let us use this operator to remove an element from the cities array of the same state.

```
>db.states.update({_id:30}, {$pop:{cities:1}})
```

This will remove the last element from the cities array. The value 1 indicates that the last/tail element of the array needs to be popped; the value -1 will remove the first element from the array. Go ahead, find the document and see which element has been popped out after executing the above update. It should be the city Mangan that would get removed.

We at times might be interested in removing certain values from the array rather than the head and tail of it. The $pull and $pullAll can be used to achieve this. Let us execute the following update which removes the city Pelling, which is in the middle of the cities array:

```
> db.states.update({_id:30}, {$pull:{cities:"Pelling"}})
```

This will remove all the elements from the array with the value provided. In this case, the string was present only once, but if it was present multiple times, all of them would have been removed. The $pullAll operator on other hand can be used to remove multiple values from the array and accepts the array of values to remove rather than a single value.

There are some more operators used for updating the documents. Refer to the operators at http://docs.mongodb.org/manual/reference/operators/#update for more details.

Before we finish off with the inserts and updates let me tell you that the update function takes two more parameters of boolean type. The general form of an update is as follows:

```
> db.<collection>.update(query, object, [Is upsert], [Is Multi Update])
```

We have away used the first two parameters as the remaining two parameters default to false. The third parameter is for `upsert`. It means Update + Insert all in an atomic operation. Let us consider the following update:

```
> db.states.update({_id:31, state:"GOA"},{$set:{cities:["Panjim"]}})
```

This update intends to update the cities field of the document whose `_id` is 31 and `state` is GOA. But since the document doesn't exist in the first place nothing will be updated. Let us change this update to the one given as follows. We just add another parameter which is a boolean value, `true`.

```
> db.states.update({_id:31, state:"GOA"},{$set:{cities:["Panjim"]}}, true)
```

Now try querying the database with the following query:

```
> db.states.find({_id:31, state:"GOA"})
```

You should see one document. What `upsert` does is, try to find a document with the given query and apply the update on it if one exists. If however, there is no document matching the given query, then insert the document given in the query (the first parameter of update) and execute the update on this inserted document and all this is done atomically.

Finally let us see what the fourth parameter means. By default an update, unlike in relational database, in Mongo always updates the first matching document and not all the documents that match the given query (first parameter). To enforce an update to all the matches, we need to explicitly provide this parameter and the value should be provided as true.

We are now done with Create, Read, and Update of documents. What's remaining is Delete. Generally the delete takes the following form:

```
> db.<collection>.remove(query, [ Remove first document only?])
```

The method to delete is `remove` and not delete. What this method does is, remove all the documents that match the query in absence of the second parameter or its value is false. If the second parameter is provided and its value is true (or 1). Then only the first document that matches the given query is deleted.

Update by default only updates the first matching document for the given query. It will update all the documents only if the fourth parameter's value to update function is true(or 1). On the other hand, remove will remove *all* the documents matching the given query by default unless you explicitly ask to remove only the first matching document for the given query by passing its value as true(or 1). This might be confusing but very important concept to remember.

That's it; we are done with delete operations too and have now completed all the Create, Update, Read, and Delete operations.

Design something that does not exist

In this section we will be looking at two of the crucial aspects of designing the schema for Mongo. One is about creation of indexes on a collection and another is about deciding upon various factors in designing the collections for a given use case. We start with the index creation.

Index creation

People from relational database background know what indexes are, it is used for the same purpose in Mongo. To explain in brief what an index is, it is a data structure created from a subset of fields of a document in a collection that will allow the user to search and retrieve documents in a collection quickly. Mongo uses B-trees for storing indexes internally. B-tree is basically an n-ary tree (a tree whose each node is with n children) where the data is stored in it in sorted order as we descend the tree. We will not get in the details of B-trees and a quick search on the web will give you the necessary details. Let us proceed and execute the following query on the Mongo shell. It is used to find a city called `Pune`.

```
> db.cities.find({city:"Pune"})
```

Executing this query should return you one document. Now it is interesting how this document was retrieved and how fast was it? We want to see how many documents were scanned in all to retrieve this document. We know that our cities collection has 495 cities. To get the plan of the query execution execute the below query. A query plan is nothing but some statistics about a query execution. There are various important figures and details in this statistics, which we will see next, that lets us tune things to enable faster retrieval of the result from the collections.

```
> db.cities.find({city:"Pune"}).explain()
```

```
> db.cities.find({city:"Pune"}).explain()
{
        "cursor" : "BasicCursor",
        "isMultiKey" : false,
        "n" : 1,
        "nscannedObjects" : 495,
        "nscanned" : 495,
        "nscannedObjectsAllPlans" : 495,
        "nscannedAllPlans" : 495,
        "scanAndOrder" : false,
        "indexOnly" : false,
        "nYields" : 0,
        "nChunkSkips" : 0,
        "millis" : 0,
        "indexBounds" : {

        },
        "server" : "Amol-PC:27017"
}
>
> _
```

We will see some important fields of this explain plan result. First is the `cursor` field. This shows the cursor used for the query execution. `BasicCursor` essentially means that the whole collection was scanned to retrieve the document. This is the worst thing to have for any query execution. So if we see this in the plan of our query, especially on big collections where query times are crucial, then there is a huge scope of optimization. How? Stay tuned. If an index is used for the query execution, then we should see `BtreeCursor` followed by the index name as the value of the field.

Next is the `isMultiKey` field. This field is a boolean value which indicates that if an index is used for query execution, a field used in the index has an array value. This is basically due to the fact how indexes are created if a field of type array is used in the index. Let us say we have an array of size 5 in a document. Then the index's B-tree will have 5 entries, one for each element of the array and each entry pointing to the same document.

The field n gives the number of documents returned by the query execution, in this case 1. The field `nscannedObjects` gives us the total number of documents scanned in the collection to retrieve the result of this query. In this case all the documents were scanned as there is no index in place. `scanAndOrder` field is a boolean value, and when true, tells us if records were sorted by Mongo server before returning the result or if an index was used for query execution, it was not used for sorting the results. The value will be false if the user didn't request the results to be sorted or the sort order requested in the query can be achieved using the indexes.

`millis` is the time is milliseconds to execute the query. `server` indicates the MongoDB server. We will also see the field `indexOnly` is after we see how we create indexes on a collection. To create an index on collection of cities, execute the following command:

```
> db.cities.ensureIndex({city:1})
```

This creates an index on one field, `city` and the value 1 indicates that the index is sorted in ascending order. Let us see how this index creation helped us in improving the performance of the query. We see the query plan again. Execute the following query:

```
> db.cities.find({city:"Pune"}).explain()
```

```
> db.cities.find({city:"Pune"}).explain()
{
        "cursor" : "BtreeCursor city_1",
        "isMultiKey" : false,
        "n" : 1,
        "nscannedObjects" : 1,
        "nscanned" : 1,
        "nscannedObjectsAllPlans" : 1,
        "nscannedAllPlans" : 1,
        "scanAndOrder" : false,
        "indexOnly" : false,
        "nYields" : 0,
        "nChunkSkips" : 0,
        "millis" : 0,
        "indexBounds" : {
                "city" : [
                        [
                                "Pune",
                                "Pune"
                        ]
                ]
        },
        "server" : "Amol-PC:27017"
}
>
>
```

As we can see in the preceding screenshot, there is a significant improvement and just one document was scanned and returned, thanks to the index created on the city field. You may be wondering why was the order of the index provided when we created an index. It doesn't make much sense when you are returning the documents in the natural order or if the index is on a single field as in this case. But if you are sorting the result set of a multi field index or compound index, the sort order does matter. For example if we have created a compound index on two fields x and y of any document as follows {x:1, y:-1}, then we are creating an index with x in ascending order and y in descending order. If your query uses a sort function then creating an index with the order same as your sort function requests the sort of these two fields will give you better query performance. Generally, index is used to get a reference to the document and then another IO operation fetches the entire document that is returned as a result of the user query. Though indexes make query fast, there is still some room for optimization. If you are not interested in the entire document and just interested in some fields and there is an index available with these fields, then use projection to just select a subset of these fields. In this case we have an index on city, so let us write a query that will fetch just the city field of the document. Execute the following query and we should see just the field in the result document:

```
> db.cities.find({city:"Pune"},{_id:0, city:1})
```

Now, let's execute and explain plan using the following:

```
> db.cities.find({city:"Pune"},{_id:0, city:1}).explain()
```

```
> db.cities.find({city:"Pune"},{_id:0, city:1})
{ "city" : "Pune" }
> db.cities.find({city:"Pune"},{_id:0, city:1}).explain()
{
        "cursor" : "BtreeCursor city_1",
        "isMultiKey" : false,
        "n" : 1,
        "nscannedObjects" : 1,
        "nscanned" : 1,
        "nscannedObjectsAllPlans" : 1,
        "nscannedAllPlans" : 1,
        "scanAndOrder" : false,
        "indexOnly" : true,
        "nYields" : 0,
        "nChunkSkips" : 0,
        "millis" : 0,
        "indexBounds" : {
                "city" : [
                        [
                                "Pune",
                                "Pune"
                        ]
                ]
        },
        "server" : "Amol-PC:27017"
}
>
> _
```

We can see that the value of the field `indexOnly` is `true`. This indicates that the result of the query was provided only by accessing the index and the IO operation to access the entire document as in case where we selected the whole document is avoided getting the result even more quickly. Such queries where the result can be covered using the fields in the index only are known as covered queries.

 Only one index is used for a query out of multiple indexes and an appropriate index is chosen automatically by the query optimizer. You may choose to tell MongoDB to use a particular index using the hint method. Generally we let the query optimizer choose one automatically and not specify one explicitly. More information on hints can be found here `http://docs.mongodb.org/manual/reference/method/cursor.hint/#cursor.hint`. Also, for query to be covered you need to choose the fields those are present in the index that is used for query execution. You cannot choose fields from different indexes in a projection and expect the query to be covered.

There is however no free lunch, though indexes improve the query performance they slow down inserts and updates, hence you need to be very careful while creating indexes and create only those you would need else there is an additional overhead to update all the relevant indexes on insert and update of documents. If you are doing a bulk import operation it is better to drop the index and recreate them after the import is complete as that would be a faster option.

Designing the collections

Let's try modeling a simple scenario. Throughout this book we have used the census schema to perform various queries, now we will look at a different scenario of an online education application which will help us design look at some the schema designing concepts. The description of the case we are trying to model is as follows.

Design the schema for an online education system. System will contain multiple courses put up by various universities and each of them will span over a few weeks. Students can enroll for various courses where they view the videos/slides uploaded and submit their assignments periodically before the deadline. Their scores will be recorded and they will be added to the final examination score at the end of the course which decides whether the student has passed or failed. Each course will be conducted by one or more lecturers.

The requirement is not too complex and we will not get deep into it and focus on some minute details. We first model this in a relational database and then in Mongo. I am assuming that many of us have come from a relational database background. When asked to design this use case in a relational database we will come up with an excellent schema design. However, when designing with Mongo we need to think different and not in a way how we might do it in a relational model. The schema design we will be doing below will serve as an example and shows exactly where the two differ so that we are in a good position to design a Mongo schema given a use case in future.

Good old relational way

Let us first try to note down the entities and then their relations.

The first entity we will have is for a Student, it should have basic details like the name, age, date she signed up, account status, and so on. We will keep things simple and leave out other additional details like the membership type, preferences, contact details, and so on. Next entity will be the `Course` entity which will contain the data about the course like the Name, the university it is offered by, the start date, and so on. A course can belong to one or more categories. This should enable students to search by the category of the course hence we will hence have a `CourseCategory` entity. There will be many lecturers conducting the course thus we shall have a `Lecturer` entity. Each course has contents and is divided in parts where new content is released weekly. The attributes of this entity is the part's name, start date, end date, and so on. Each part of the course has some content present. The content could be a link to the videos/presentation or some free text to be displayed (it could also be the video files itself saved in the database, but we will keep things simple and assume that it is a link to the video stored elsewhere (in case of videos). We will call this entity a `CourseContent` entity. Many such Course contents will be grouped into one complete course content. We will name this entity `CourseContentGroup` entity since this groups the content of the course released. There would also be a foreign key reference to the `CourseContentGroup` from `CourseContent` entity, as this content can belong to exactly one group. Each part of the course has one or more assignments associated to it. The assignment entity will contain attributes like the text describing the assignment, its due date, and so on. It will also contain a foreign key reference to the `CourseContent` entity. This entity is called `CourseAssignment`. Finally, a student submits her assignments. So we need an entity to store the answers submitted. The entity will have a foreign key reference to the student's entity telling which student this assignment belongs to and a foreign key to the `CourseAssignment` entity. We call this entity `AssignmentSubmission`.

The following image shows various entities and the relations between them:

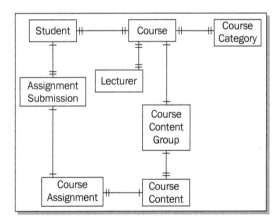

We can see there are a few many-to-many relations too which needs join tables to join these entities together. We will require join tables for Student to Course, Lecturer to Course, and a Course to CourseCategory entities. Thus we have eight entities and three join tables which sums up to 11 tables in all.

We can see how things can get complicated even for a simple use case (we have even left out a lot of minute details). The schema is not very change friendly. It is quite rigid and not flexible to accommodate new requirements and features. For example, consider we decide to add a final examination at the end of the entire course. In this case we will need to add another table to store those assignment questions. We cannot use the `CourseAssignment` table as these questions are not related to a specific `CourseContent` but to the whole course itself. Similarly, to store the answers of a student we will need another table and soon there is a table explosion. Now this is not the only way we can design the relational schema and other ways exists but those too might not be clean and need some workarounds and hacks to accommodate these changes.

The Mongo way

We have had enough discussion around the relational database design. Let us look at how to design the same use case using Mongo. We will be designing the use case using three collections. Yes, you read it right, just three collections and those are Student, Course, and Lecturer. But what about other details, where will we be fitting those in? Well, we will be keeping all those in one of the above three collections. Let's see how. We start with the simplest collection of all, the Lecturer collection. The attributes of this collection are no different than the columns of the relational database. The document looks something like this:

```
{_id:"1", name:"…", university:"…", aboutMe:"…", …}
```

Nothing extraordinary, it just contains plain simple attributes about the lecturer conducting the courses, same as those we would have in a relational database. Now the things start getting interesting. Let us take a look at a document in a Course collection:

```
{
  _id:100, name:"Introduction to MongoDB", university:"MyMongo
University",
  startDate:"01/03/2013", duration:"6 weeks",
  category:["NoSQL", "Big Data", "Database"],
  lecturers:[1, 2],
  content:[
    {name:"Week One",
      summary:"In this week we will be…..",
      lectureLink:"http://myuniv.com/....",
      assignment:{
        assignmentId:"100_C1",
        title:"Setting up MongoDB",
        marks:5,
        steps:"…"
```

```
        }
     ….
     },
     {name:"Week Two",
        summary:"In this week we will be…..",
        lectureLink:"http://myuniv.com/....",
        assignment:{
           assignmentId:"100_C2",
           title:"Querying with Mongo",
           marks:5,
           steps:"…"
        }
     ….
     },
     ….
   ],
   finalAssignment:[
     {
        assignmentId:"100_F1",
        assignmentId :""name:"Assignment One",
        marks:10,
        description:"In this assignment…"
     },
     {
        assignmentId:"100_F2",
        assignmentId :""name:"Assignment Two",
        marks:10,
        description:"In this assignment…"
     },
     ….
   ]
}
```

Ok, don't be scared by looking at the document. We will break it up now and see what it exactly does. The top five fields `_id`, `name`, `university`, `startDate`, `duration` are pretty self-explanatory and are used to give the unique course id, name of the course, the university which offers it a, start date of the course, and the duration respectively. Next, the category field, this one is an array of free text and holds various categories this course can be classified in. This will facilitate the search of various courses based on categories. Relational databases achieved using a many to many relation between `Course` and `CourseCategory` tables, which needed three tables including a join table to achieve this mapping.

The lecturer field is an array and holds an array of numbers. When we say array of numbers, we haven't defined any constraints for the field for the type it can hold at the database level but it is something we have enforced in our application. Not only this is an array of numbers, but also all the numbers act as key to the lecturer's ID in the `Lecturer` collection, this is called linking. Again there is nothing in the database to enforce this similar to having foreign key references in Relational DB. This is the integrity that the application accessing the data is supposed to enforce and maintain.

You must be wondering, what good this is then? Isn't it better to enforce the constraints as we do in the relational database? The answer is, the Mongo developers have done some research before developing the database and they found that many times applications duplicate the validations at application layer despite having constraints at database level. So it is better to let go of the constraints at database side and gain on performance and flexibility to scale the system. Now it makes sense doesn't it? Another thing we should pay attention to. Both the course to categories (the categories field) and the course to lecturer relationship (the lecturers field) are many-to-many. Yet in case of categories we have the categories specified in the array in the document, that is, embedded them in the document. For the lecturer relation however, we have linking to the documents in an external collection. Why is it so? First thing you need to remember is always prefer embedding to linking. Resort to linking only in case where it doesn't make sense to duplicate the same document in multiple documents by embedding. For example, embedding the entire lecturer's document in the lecturer's array of the course's document would not be a great idea especially since we know that the same document might be duplicated in many other courses conducted by the same lecturer. Down side of linking is, we cannot join two documents in Mongo and we need to fire separate queries from application to fetch the related, linked documents.

There is a hybrid approach though which addresses the problem of additional queries to some extent. Consider in our application we will be showing a list of courses offered, the start date, duration and who is/are the lecturer(s). With the current schema design we will have first query the course's collection and then fire another query with the distinct lecturer's ID from the retrieved courses to fetch the lecturers. We will have to then manually map the retrieved lecturer's document to the lecturer's ID in the course's documents. This is painful, verbose, does not scale well and prone to errors. A slight change in the schema can however address this problem. The idea is, rather than duplicating the entire lecturer's document across multiple course's documents, duplicate just the minimum required fields. Let us say just duplicate the lecturer's name. So after the modification the lecturer's array might look as follows:

```
lecturers:[
    {lecturerId:1, name:"Mark"},
    {lecturerId:2, name:"John"}
]
```

The above approach has duplicated the lecturer's name in the course's document as well as the lecturer's document. We still link the lecturer from the course's document but now we need to query for the entire lecturer's document only if we need additional details about the lecturer. In the preceding case where we want to show the course details summary we need not query the lecturer's collection as our course's collection now has all the information, the name of the course, start date, duration, and the lecturer's names within it. Embedding versus Linking is a very crucial decision of schema design and is relevant mostly in many-to-many relations as in the previous two cases we saw. It will also come into picture for Many to One case if we plan to keep reference to the one side on the many side.

Moving on, we look at the `content` field. This is a one-to-many relation from course's perspective and is easy to model. We simply embed the content in the course's document. The course content will never be used by any other course and hence linking doesn't make sense leaving us with embedding as the only choice. The content field's type is an array where each element of the array is a document representing a part of the entire course's content. This document which represents the part of the course in turn contain more fields like the name of the part, summary of the part, an external link to the video lectures uploaded and also the details of the assignments related to this part of the course. The assignment in turn will be another document containing the details of the assignment. When new content of the course is released all the application needs to do is add a new document representing the part of the newly releases course in the content array of the main course document in the collection. (Can you guess how? We have looked at this operator in an early section of the book).

Finally, the `finalAssignment` field is an array that contains multiple documents. Each one is an assignment that will be a part of the final exam of the course. Now if you recall, in the relational database after the schema was designed accommodating the change to incorporate the final assignments with the course, we needed some more tables and more joins between them. In Mongo it was as simple as adding an additional field in the course's document. That's the beauty of the schemaless feature of Mongo. That covers the course document. We will quickly look at the student's document without getting into many details as the concepts for designing this is same as what we did for the course's document.

```
{
    _id:111,
    name:"Jack",
    dateOfBirth:"…",
    aboutMe:"..",
    website:"..",
    email:"…",
    …

    coursesEnrolled:[
      {courseId:100, name:" Introduction to MongoDB"},
        …
```

```
    ],
    assignmentSubmissions:[
      {assignmentId:"100_C1",   answer:…},
      {assignmentId:"100_F1",   answer:…},
        …
    ]

  }
```

The preceding student document now must be looking convincing and easy to you'll after seeing the course's document in detail, isn't it? Let us see how we have structured it. The field name, `dateOfBirth`, `aboutMe`, `website`, `email` are self-explanatory and the values are simple string values except for the `dateOfBirth` field which is a date field. Next two fields, the `coursesEnrolled` and `assignmentSubmissions` are arrays of documents and give us the information about the courses the student has enrolled to and various assignment submissions. This was achieved in relational database by having many-to-many relation between `Student` and `Course` table and `Student` and `CourseAssignment` table respectively. This needed a total of three master tables and two join tables to perform the job, which is achieved using just two fields in the student's collection. The `coursesEnrolled` could have been an array of string values where each value links to a `courseId` in the course's document. But we chose an approach we discussed earlier and decided to add the name of the course along with the `courseId` and make the individual elements in an array a document rather than a simple string value. This enables us to show in the student's profile page the names of the courses the student has enrolled for without firing additional queries on the course's document to retrieve just the course's name for, the summary of the profile. But remember, in case of scenarios where the name of the course has changed, you need to update two collections as the name of the course is redundantly stored in the student's document as well.

For the `assignmentSubmission` field, we have an array with documents storing the assignment id and the answer to the assignment. As you must have observed, we have chosen to use the same field for storing both the final assignment and the assignments given at the end of a part of the course. That is because both these assignments have a different format for ID and we can distinguish this based on the appropriate question this answer is for. You may also choose to have two separate fields in the student's document to store the final assignment and the assignment related to a part of the course.

Another important aspect to consider is, what is to be done for the history? The student possibly has enrolled for many courses in the past and has submitted a lots of assignments. Do we store all that in the student's document? The trouble with that is, the document will get bigger and bigger over a period of time and we will have face some performance issues and also the maximum size of the document is 16MB, which is huge. A better idea is to have some sort of jobs setup that will remove the data of the historical courses and the assignment related to those from the student's document and move it to another collection meant for archival. The structure of the document in this archival collection can be same as the students' collection or can be completely different. The idea is to keep the documents in the students' collection as lean as possible and not allow them to grow fat.

Phew, that was quite a lot of reading to do trying to tell what needs to done for the schema designing. With that we have finished the most important aspects of schema design.

It's all about grouping things

We have so far seen how to query the collections in Mongo, various operators that can be used to query the collection, how documents can be inserted or removed from collections, and how to update the documents with the help of various update operators. How many of you'll have asked this question to yourself, "How do I perform aggregation operations with these operators?" Lots of you, right? For those who have not and are not sure what aggregation is, it is simply a way of aggregating the results based on the documents in the collection. For those who are from Relational world, it is the counterpart in Mongo of the famous **group by** in RDBMS. Ok then, let us start off and see how to perform this aggregation in Mongo.

There are a couple of ways to aggregate the data. One is a simple lightweight way which was first introduced in Version 2.2 of Mongo and another has been around for quite some time, slightly heavy but extremely powerful. The lightweight approach is called **aggregation framework** and the heavy one is **Map reduce**. We start by looking at aggregation framework first. We introduce the basic concepts; introduce seven operators (called pipeline operators) we can use with aggregation framework and apply them on our census database to demonstrate various concepts.

The aggregation framework

All the aggregation performed on a collection is performed using the `aggregate` wrapper function on the collection. Suppose we want to perform aggregation on a collection `mycollection`, then our aggregation operation will be done using the following command:

```
>db.mycollection.aggregate([opr 1, opr 2, ... opr n])
```

The parameter taken in the square bracket is called a pipeline of operators; you may optionally skip the square brackets and pass the comma separated operators to achieve the same result. Each operator performs an operation on the incoming data and passes it on to the next operator in the pipe. This is analogous to pipes in Unix, where output of one process is routed as input of another process through the pipe. Each operator based on its behavior will either output a larger number of documents, smaller number of documents or same number of documents than its input. The result of the `aggregate` function is a JSON document which contains a field called `result` whose value is an array where each element of the array is the result of the last pipeline aggregation operator in the pipeline of operators. This description is enough to scratch the surface and get us started. We will next see the seven types of pipeline aggregation operators and finally perform some operations on the census database to yield interesting results.

Next we shall see the pipeline operators.

The project operator ($project)

This operator outputs the same number of documents as the number fed to it. Its primary purpose is, output a limited number of fields from its input document, rename the fields in the output document, and introduce computed fields in the output document. Let us see some examples of its usage. The following command will just select the name of the state and the _id field of the state's document. Providing {state:1, _id:1} ensures that the documents outputted (or passed to next operator in pipeline) contains just these two fields.

```
> db.states.aggregate({$project:{state:1, _id:1}})
```

The following screenshot shows a part of the output of the above command:

```
> db.states.aggregate({{$project:{state:1, _id:1}})
<
        "result" : [
                {
                        "_id" : 1,
                        "state" : "ANDAMAN & NICOBAR ISLANDS"
                },
                {
                        "_id" : 2,
                        "state" : "ANDHRA PRADESH"
                },
                {
                        "_id" : 3,
                        "state" : "ASSAM"
                },
                {
                        "_id" : 4,
                        "state" : "BIHAR"
                },
                {
                        "_id" : 5,
                        "state" : "CHANDIGARH"
                },
```

The size of the result array of this operation will be 31 as there are 31 states in all in this collection. Consider the following aggregation query using $project:

```
> db.states.aggregate({
   $project:{state:1, _id:0, capital:"$info.capital"}
})
```

This query will project the state's name and an additional field called capital whose value is the value of the capital field inside the info field's document if one exists. It is interesting to see how we accessed the info field in the input document as $info. We just access the top-level document in that manner. Any nested field is accessed using the dot(.) followed by the path to the field we want to access. To elaborate further on this suppose the input document is as follows (we have not included all the fields for clarity):

```
{_id:15, state:"MAHARASHTRA"... info:{area:307713, capital:"Mumbai",
...}}
```

The output of the project operation for this state will be as follows:

```
{"state":"MAHARASHTRA", "capital":"Mumbai"}
```

The match operation ($match)

This operator is primarily used to filter out the documents that will be passed on to the next pipeline operator in chain or to the final output. The general structure for this operator is as follows:

```
> db.collection.aggregate({$match:{<expression>}})
```

This will pass the document to the next operator in pipeline if the expression evaluates to true. Let us see an example. We will use the match operator to select all the cities which have the word Mumbai in it.

```
> db.cities.aggregate({$match:{city:/Mumbai/i}})
```

This command should output a result with three documents for cities in it. It is recommended that the match operator should be placed high up in the pipeline to limit the documents to be processed by the operators lower in the pipeline. Placing the operator on the top of the pipeline can also make use of the index on a collection efficiently.

The limit operator ($limit)

The limit operator simply limits the number of documents that pass through it through the pipeline. The operator is expressed as follows:

```
> db.collection.aggregate({$limit:<number to limit>})
```

Thus doing;

```
> db.cities.aggregate({$limit:15})
```

The preceding operation will restrict the output to just the top 15 documents from the cities collection. This is pretty simple operator and will not modify the documents before they are sent to the next operator in the pipeline. Once the number of documents specified within the limit operator has passed the operator in the pipeline, all the remaining documents are skipped and not passed further down.

The skip operator ($skip)

This operator skips the first n number of documents passing this operator in the pipeline. Once the given number of documents is skipped, all the remaining documents are passed. This is exactly opposite to the limit operator we saw previously. The operator is expressed as follows:

```
> db.collection.aggregate({$skip:<number to skip>})
```

Thus doing:

```
> db.cities.aggregate({$skip:10})
```

The above operation will skip the first 10 documents coming from the pipeline to this operator and then allow all other documents reaching this document in the pipeline.

The unwind operator ($unwind)

This is an interesting operator and to be used with array operators only. When used with an array field of size n in a document, it passes down the pipeline n documents where it takes the individual element in the array field, create a document with all the remaining fields in the incoming document, sticks this single value from the array in the same field as the one which carried the array, and passes it down the pipeline. This is done for all the elements in the array thus generating n documents. Confused? Ok, No problem, lets us take a look at an example.

We first look at a state in the states collection with the name KERALA. The query to see this state's document is as follows:

```
>db.states.findOne({state:"KERALA"})
```

On executing this query you should see 7 cities in the cities array. We will do an unwind operation on the cities field of the document for state kerala as follows:

```
> db.states.aggregate({$match:{state:"KERALA"}}, {$unwind:"$cities"})
```

One thing to note here is that we have a pipeline of two aggregation operators here, first one will match just the state with name KERALA and second will perform the unwind operation on the cities field of the document passed by the match operator (which is one document for the state of Kerala). We specify the name of the field to the unwind operator using a $ followed by the name of the field in the document, in this case $cities. On executing the previous command we should get seven documents in the result, one for each element in the cities field. For the state of Kerala we have the following seven cities in the array, Kozhikode, Palakkad, Thrissur, Kochi, Alappuza, Kollam, and Thiruvananthapuram (yes, I know it's a very long name). The result of the aggregation operation will be:

```
{_id:13, state:"KERALA", cities:"Kozhikode", info:{...}},
{_id:13, state:"KERALA", cities:"Palakkad", info:{...}}
...
{_id:13, state:"KERALA", cities:"Thiruvananthapuram", info:{...}}
```

I have skipped the four documents for simplicity and taken the liberty to show them as ellipses. The info field is also not shown as that is exactly identical to the one in the original state's document given as input to the unwind operator. The interesting bit is the cities field. This field in the original input document was of type array, in the output document however, has it as a string with the value same as individual elements of the original input array thus giving us seven documents. Now that we are clear with the unwind operator let's move ahead with the next operator.

The sort operator ($sort)

The sort pipeline operator simply sorts the incoming documents by the field and the order you mention before sending it down the pipeline. Period. It is pretty simple to use this operator too. Let's see with an example where we want to sort the documents by descending order of the names of the states.

```
> db.states.aggregate({$sort:{state:-1}})
```

The operator is expressed as $sort followed by the document mentioning the field by which to order and whether to sort by ascending or descending order. In this case the name of the field is state and the order is descending, which is specified by -1. To sort in an ascending order we give the order as 1.

 The sort operation sorts the data in memory and hence you need to be extra careful with the size of the data that flows in to sort operator and provide it with the bare minimum documents you need to accomplish the task.

The group operator ($group)

This is perhaps the most important aggregation pipeline operator and is synonymous to the group by clause of the Relational world. It is used to perform the functions on the documents. The output is dependent on the group we specify, similar to the way we specify the column names in the group by clause. The group is specified with the field called _id and we can have the aggregation result in another field in the resulting output document. Let us look at an example to make it clear. We have our cities collection which has the state's name in each document too. The idea is to perform an aggregation operation on this collection grouping the cities based on the states and then finding the count of cities in each state. We basically want to group by the state name and find the count in each. To perform this operation we execute the following query:

```
> db.cities.aggregate({$group:{_id:"$state", count:{$sum:1}}})
```

Since the aggregation we would be performing is group, we have the $group operator mentioned in the JSON query. What's more interesting is the JSON document provided as the value. This document has two fields _id and count. The _id field is mandatory for the $group operator and is used to give the field of the incoming document that we wish to group on. In this case the state field. This field is mentioned using a $ followed by the name of the field, in this case $state. The count field is a field we define and expect the count of the grouped by states and present in the output. The name of the field is any arbitrary name. You can choose it to be abc, xyz, and so on but it has to be meaningful. The value of this field is interesting. It is a document {$sum:1} which adds up 1 each time a state's name is encountered in the grouping so in the end we achieve a count which is same as the number or times the state's name appeared in the list of documents provided. This is analogous to the count () or sum () in a Relational world. Where did this $sum operator come from? We haven't seen it so far, isn't it?

The answer is, there are quite a few operators performing operations for counting, summing, finding average, comparison, mathematical operations like adding, subtracting, dividing, and multiplying, string operations, and so on. We will not be explaining them all in detail here and you can refer to them whenever you need them from the documentation provided here `http://docs.mongodb.org/manual/reference/operator/` just lookout for the aggregation operators sub section on this page.

It is also possible that we group by more than one field and in that case the value of the `_id` field is a document rather than a simple string as in this case. For example, if we want to group by two fields a and b in a document we would have the id field as `_id:{a:"$a", b:"$b"}`.

Let us now put these operators to use for a sample scenario. The scenario is as follows:

Scenario

You have the states collection containing various documents for the states. Each state has an array of cities in it. You need to find out the number of cities grouped by their first alphabet of the name and find the top three most common starting alphabets of the cities.

Analysis

The names of the cities have to be sourced from the array in the state's document. So we will use the **unwind** operator on the cities array of the state. We will need a **project** operation that will pass on the first character of each of the city's name to the next operator in the pipeline which will **group** them based on that character and later sort them before **limiting** the output to just top three results.

The words marked in bold give us a clue on various pipeline operators we will use to find the result. Let us then try writing the aggregation pipeline for this query.

```
> db.states.aggregate(
    {$project:{cities:1, _id:0}},
    {$unwind:"$cities"},
    {$project:{first:{$substr:["$cities", 0 , 1]}}},
    {$group:{_id:"$first", count:{$sum:1}}},
    {$sort:{count:-1}},
    {$limit:3}
)
```

On executing the preceding command we see the result as shown in the following screenshot. It seems that B, K, and S are the top three first alphabets of the names of the cities.

```
> db.states.aggregate(
...     ($project:(cities:1, _id:0)),
...     ($unwind:"$cities"),
...     ($project:(first:($substr:["$cities", 0 , 1]))),
...     ($group:(_id:"$first", count:($sum:1))),
...     ($sort:(count:-1)),
...     ($limit:3)
... )
{
        "result" : [
                {
                        "_id" : "B",
                        "count" : 74
                },
                {
                        "_id" : "K",
                        "count" : 43
                },
                {
                        "_id" : "S",
                        "count" : 42
                }
        ],
        "ok" : 1
}
>
>
```

If you look at our statement in the analysis before we wrote the aggregation command you
will notice a one-to-one match between the flow we analyzed and the operators we put in
the pipeline. Just a couple of thing worth mentioning are, the first project operator is optional
and we put it just to ensure that only the bare minimum fields needed are passed down the
pipeline and the group operator uses the $substr operator to find the first alphabet of the
city's name. You should find the description of this operator in the operator's reference link we
provided earlier.

Isn't it easy to use the aggregation framework to perform the aggregation operations? There
are a couple of caveats though which I feel are worth mentioning. The aggregation operations
can produce a maximum of 16MB of output data per pipeline. The data exceeding this value will
produce an error. Similarly operations consuming more than 10 percent of CPU will produce
an error. But as we discussed earlier, it is a lightweight alternative to the heavy Map-reduce
operations. If you are struck with the data volumes and CPU usage problems then Map reduce,
which we will see next is the only alternative.

Aggregation using Map reduce

The concept of Map reduce is slightly complicated and might be slightly difficult to digest
initially for novice developers but once you understand the crux of it, it is simple. Though
explaining what Map reduce is out of the scope of this book, we still will have a quick
introduction to it.

Map reduce is a programming model for working on large data sets and was invented by Google. Map reduce involves breaking down the problem in a key value pairs for processing. So if your problem can be broken down into key value pair, you can use Map reduce. The two phases in Map reduce as the name suggests, are map phase and the reduce phase. In the map phase we emit key and value pairs from the input dataset. The data emitted from the map function is called intermediate data in map reduce terminology. In reduce phase we process this intermediate data to generate the final output result. The data passed to reduce phase however is not the one that is the direct output of Map phase but it is the key that is emitted from map phase and a list of values where values are those emitted for the same key in the map phase. The details about Map reduce can be found in the research paper by Google `http://research.google.com/archive/mapreduce.html`.

Do not worry if this doesn't make a lot of sense for now. We will implement the same problem we implemented using the aggregation framework and compare the output for both of them. Before we begin let us see how do we actually perform Map reduce in Mongo.

The first activity to do is to implement the map and reduce JavaScript functions. These functions execute on the Mongo server for the data set we wish to run Map reduce on. Second we invoke Map reduce on a collection as follows:

```
> db.<collection>.mapReduce (
        mapFunction,
        reduceFunction,
        options
 )
```

Let us see what those options are. The options are mentioned as a JSON document and the following are the valid recognized values:

```
{
out: <collection>,
query: <document>,
sort: <document>,
limit: <number>,
finalize: <function>,
scope: <document>,
jsMode: <boolean>,
verbose: <boolean>
}
```

Let us see what those values are. These descriptions might not make a lot of sense immediately but once we see an example later it should hopefully be clearer. Of all the options mentioned, out is the only mandatory option we need to provide.

- ✦ out: Used to specify the location of the result of the Map reduce operation. The value, if a string is taken as the collection to which the result is written. To output the result of the small map reduce jobs you can write the output inline to the console. This is done by setting the value of this field to {inline:1}.

- ✦ query: The query that will be executed on the input collection to provide the input to the map function.

- ✦ sort: The sort function will be applied to the input data before it is provided to the map function. This can be done for a couple of reasons. First is to sort the data as per the emit key used by the map function to reduce the number of reduce operations, and secondly it can be used with the limit option to provide a subset of the sorted data to the map function.

- ✦ finalize: A JavaScript function that will follow the reduce function and modify its output. The finalize method receives two values, the key and the value returned by the reduce function.

- ✦ scope: Specifies the global variables available to map, reduce, and finalize functions.

- ✦ jsMode: Specifies whether the intermediate data needs to be converted to BSON before passing to the reduce function.

- ✦ verbose: Indicates whether the timing information should be provided with the output, defaults to true.

Just to recap the scenario we implemented using the aggregation framework, here it is once again.

Scenario

You have the states collection containing various documents for the states. Each state has an array of cities in it. You need to find out the number of cities grouped by their first alphabet of the name and find the top three most common starting alphabets of the cities.

We start by implementing the map and reduce functions. Execute the following code on your shell:

```
> function map() {
  for(i = 0; i < this.cities.length; i++) {
    emit(this.cities[i].substring(0,1), 1);
  }
}
```

```
> function reduce(key, values) {
    return Array.sum(values)
}
```

The map function simply emits the key as the first character of the city and a value 1. But as you can see we are referring to the cities as `this.cities`. Where is this cities field coming from? The answer is the map function gets applied for each and every document in the collection. What does this exactly mean? Let us see a very simple example in JavaScript. Consider the following method:

```
> function f() {print(this.a + " and " this.b);}
```

Now if you just execute this function on the console you should see the following:

```
> undefined and undefined
```

That undefined is for `this.a` and `this.b`. To get a proper meaning to this function execute the following line:

```
> f.apply({a:1, b:2})
```

Now you should see:

```
> 1 and 2
```

We don't want to explain a lot of JavaScript here but this is to tell you that Mongo does something similar on your provided map function for each and every document in the collection. This you can access the fields of the document directly using `this`. Getting back to the map function, we simply emit the first character of the city and a number 1 which indicates the count for character emitted. Hence there will be as many number of 1's emitted per character as the number of times it was encountered in the city's first character. This is pretty simple and straight forward.

Now for the reduce function. This function accepts two parameters, first is the key and second is a list of values. The key has the same value that we emit from the map function. The value however is the array of values emitted in the map function for the same key or the value returned by a previous invocation of the reduce function for the same key. Yes, it is possible that the reduce function might be invoked multiple times for the same key in which case the list of values will contain the previously returned value for the reduce function. This effectively means that the value returned from the reduce function should be identical to the one emitted in the map function. These values can be anything as simple as a number as we did in this case or can be a complex object containing multiple attributes.

Let us execute the Map reduce operation now. The result of the Map reduce operation can be directed to a collection as we saw earlier using the out `config` parameter. We will send the output of this Map reduce operation to the collection named `census_mr`. Invoke the Map reduce as follows:

```
> db.states.mapReduce(map, reduce, {out:"census_mr"})
```

We see something like the following on executing the operation and it seems that our operation is successful:

```
> db.states.mapReduce(map, reduce, {out:"census_mr"})
{
        "result" : "census_mr",
        "timeMillis" : 154,
        "counts" : {
                "input" : 31,
                "emit" : 498,
                "reduce" : 23,
                "output" : 23
        },
        "ok" : 1,
}
>
>
```

Our results have gone to the census_mr collection and a quick query of this collection shows us various documents with an _id field whose value is the starting character of the city's name and a field value whose value is a number which gives the number of occurrence of the character. We are interested in the top three values. Hence let us execute the following query:

```
> db.census_mr.find().sort({value:-1}).limit(3)
```

The output of this query is as follows:

```
> db.census_mr.find().sort({value:-1}).limit(3)
{ "_id" : "B", "value" : 74 }
{ "_id" : "K", "value" : 43 }
{ "_id" : "S", "value" : 42 }
>
```

As we see the previous results we achieved using Map reduce are the same as what we achieved using aggregation.

Obvious question one will have in mind is when to use Map reduce and when to use aggregation framework. The rule of thumb is, if you have Mongo 2.2 and above, and your requirement is simple then use aggregation framework. Fall back to Map Reduce only for pre 2.2 Mongo deployment or the requirement needs a lot of computations and math, something too complex to be expressed in aggregation framework. Map reduce is ultimately JavaScript code and hence a better choice where complex computations are involved.

The map function can invoke the emit function as many times it wants. An important thing to remember for both map and reduce functions is that it cannot access the database for any reason and should have no impact outside the map function additionally the reduce function should be idempotent.

Typical Map reduce operation includes the following four steps:

1. Read the input collection.
2. Execute the map operation.
3. Execute the reduce operation.
4. Write to output collection.

For reading the collection, Mongo takes a read lock on the input collection which it yields after every 100 document reads. The JavaScript functions `map`, `reduce`, and `finalize` takes a JavaScript lock not allowing any other script to execute in parallel. The JavaScript execution is single threaded and since `map`, `reduce`, and `finalize` functions are typically executed quickly and yield lock periodically allowing interleaving of execution of other functions, they all appear to run in parallel.

Summary

We have seen a significant number of important features of Mongo in this section. As a developer, if you are well versed with the features we have seen so far, then I believe you are battle ready and can look at implementing your project using Mongo. However, what we have seen in this section is from a shell and rarely any application uses shell for its work. What we need are drivers for various programming languages which will allow us to perform the previous activities from the application. Mongo has drivers are various platforms and you may take a look at them at this link `http://docs.mongodb.org/ecosystem/drivers/`.

People and places you should get to know

If you need help with MongoDB, following are the sites and resources you should find invaluable.

Official sites

- Homepage: `http://www.mongodb.org/`
- Official MongoDB documentation: `http://docs.mongodb.org/manual/`
- Official issues and features tracker: `https://jira.mongodb.org/`
- Official mailing list: `http://groups.google.com/group/mongodb-announce`

Articles and tutorials

- The MongoDB operator reference page is something to be bookmarked as it would be widely used in many scenarios: `http://docs.mongodb.org/manual/reference/operator/`
- 10Gen is the company behind MongoDB and offers commercial support too. The company's URL: `http://www.10gen.com/`
- A collection of white papers can be found here: `http://www.10gen.com/datasheets-and-white-papers`
- An exceptionally large archive of presentations on MongoDB will be found at: `http://www.10gen.com/presentations`
- Every now and then 10 Gen conducts some free online courses on Mongo. You may watch out for them at: `https://education.10gen.com/`
- Get an overview of some of the Mongo's production deployments here: `http://www.mongodb.org/about/production-deployments/`
- A couple of interactive MongoDB tutorials can be found here: `http://mongly.openmymind.net/tutorial/index` and `http://try.mongodb.org/`

Community

- Official MongoDB blog: `http://blog.mongodb.org/`
- Stackoverflow forum and questions on MongoDB can be found here: `http://stackoverflow.com/questions/tagged/mongodb`

Twitter

- Follow MongoDB on `@MongoDB`
- Follow 10Gen on `@10gen`

About Packt Publishing

Packt, pronounced 'packed', published its first book "*Mastering phpMyAdmin for Effective MySQL Management*" in April 2004 and subsequently continued to specialize in publishing highly focused books on specific technologies and solutions.

Our books and publications share the experiences of your fellow IT professionals in adapting and customizing today's systems, applications, and frameworks. Our solution based books give you the knowledge and power to customize the software and technologies you're using to get the job done. Packt books are more specific and less general than the IT books you have seen in the past. Our unique business model allows us to bring you more focused information, giving you more of what you need to know, and less of what you don't.

Packt is a modern, yet unique publishing company, which focuses on producing quality, cutting-edge books for communities of developers, administrators, and newbies alike. For more information, please visit our website: www.packtpub.com.

Writing for Packt

We welcome all inquiries from people who are interested in authoring. Book proposals should be sent to author@packtpub.com. If your book idea is still at an early stage and you would like to discuss it first before writing a formal book proposal, contact us; one of our commissioning editors will get in touch with you.

We're not just looking for published authors; if you have strong technical skills but no writing experience, our experienced editors can help you develop a writing career, or simply get some additional reward for your expertise.

Ruby and MongoDB Web Development Beginner's Guide

ISBN: 978-1-84951-502-3   Paperback: 332 pages

Create dynamic web applications by combining the power of Ruby and MongoDB

1. Step-by-step instructions and practical examples to creating web applications with Ruby and MongoDB

2. Learn to design the object model in a NoSQL way

3. Create objects in Ruby and map them to MongoDB

PHP and MongoDB Web Development Beginner's Guide

ISBN: 978-1-84951-362-3   Paperback: 292 pages

Combine the power of PHP and MongoDB to build dynamic web 2.0 applications

1. Learn to build PHP-powered dynamic web applications using MongoDB as the data backend

2. Handle user sessions, store real-time site analytics, build location-aware web apps, and much more, all using MongoDB and PHP

3. Full of step-by-step instructions and practical examples, along with challenges to test and improve your knowledge

Please check **www.PacktPub.com** for information on our titles

Opa Application Development

ISBN: 978-1-78216-374-9   Paperback: 116 pages

A rapid and secure web development framework to develop web applications quickly and easily in Opa

1. Discover the Opa framework in a progressive and structured way

2. Build secure, powerful web applications with Opa.

3. Create three complete web application demos with Opa.

CouchDB and PHP Web Development Beginner's Guide

ISBN: 978-1-84951-358-6   Paperback: 304 pages

Get your PHP application from conception to deployment by leveraging CouchDB's robust features

1. Explore the Processing language with a broad range of practical recipes for computational art and graphics

2. Wide coverage of topics including interactive art, computer vision, visualization, drawing in 3D, and much more with Processing

3. Create interactive art installations and learn to export your artwork for print, screen, Internet, and mobile devices

Please check **www.PacktPub.com** for information on our titles

www.ingramcontent.com/pod-product-compliance
Lightning Source LLC
Chambersburg PA
CBHW060205060326
40690CB00018B/4264